Muslims in Northern Ireland

*Contributions and achievements
with a historical introduction*

Moira McCombe
Dr. M.M. Khan

Published by
Al-Nisa Association Northern Ireland

Copyright Al-Nisa Association Northern Ireland 2005

c/o 46 Mount Eden Park, Belfast, BT9 6RB

Designed and Printed in Northern Ireland by Three Creative Company Limited.

ISBN 0-9551493-0-4
ISBN 978-0-9551493-0-6

Foreword

Mrs. A.S. Khan

The Al-Nisa Association N.I was set up in 1998 as an independent organisation to support Muslim women in Northern Ireland. The organisation is managed and organised by women who are all volunteers.

As an organisation representing Muslim women in Northern Ireland we are aware of additional efforts needed by our community, other minority ethnic communities and the local community to promote integration, especially after long years of troubles which have affected all sections of society in Northern Ireland.

This publication has been a dream of mine and of Al-Nisa for many years.

Through this book we wish to promote the positive aspects of integration of Muslims into the society of Northern Ireland, briefly describe the history of the Muslim community in Ireland over the past 200 years and celebrate the positive aspects of the ethnically diverse community which Northern Ireland is becoming.

In order to give a true representation of the diversity of the local Muslim community, we have tried to incorporate interviews with Muslims from a variety of the many social and professional backgrounds within our community. We have also tried to achieve a balance of gender, age, geographical spread and national/ethnic background.

In recent times there has been a rise of racially motivated attacks in Northern Ireland and a lot of negative press about Northern Ireland across Europe as a result. As a community we welcome the legislation which has been introduced in Northern Ireland to combat this type of criminal activity and to promote justice and equality. The 'Race Equality Strategy for Northern Ireland' and the 'Shared Future' policy are also welcome steps in promoting good relations and tackling racism in society.

Over the years the majority of Muslims have had very positive experiences in Northern Ireland and have integrated and contributed towards uplifting their communities. As an organisation we felt that it was important to highlight the positive role played by many Muslims in further promoting the existing good relations between members of all communities and their positive contribution to Northern Ireland made over the past 70 years.

Second and third generations of Muslims are now being born and brought up in Northern Ireland and are very valuable members of our society. We hope that, through this book, they can appreciate how welcoming and supportive many individuals and organisations have been and continue to be in Northern Ireland, and also how the achievements of the Muslim community have improved the lives of many people in Northern Ireland as a whole.

Mrs. A.S.Khan MBE
Chairperson; Al-Nisa Associations N.I

Acknowledgements

Al-Nisa Association N.I would like to acknowledge the contributions of the following individuals and organisations in the publication of this book.

Belfast City Council
Brighton History centre, Museum and Art Gallery
(Ms. Donna Steele and Mr. Paul Jordan)
Community Relations Council
Interfaith Forum
Northern Ireland Council for Ethnic Minorities
OFMDFM – Gender Equality Unit
OFMDFM – Racial Equality Unit
Plate 1. Courtesy of Shakespeare Institute, University of Birmingham
PSNI
Queen's University Belfast
Stranmillis College
Voluntary Services Bureau

The Al-Nisa Executive Committee members
Contributions from the Community & Interviewees
Dr Mazhar Khan (Consultant Cardiologist) for his input
Moira McCombe
Gabrielle Doherty
Sean Kelly
Eileen McCombe
Andrew Dunlop
Marc Steenson & Paul McDonnell from Three Creative Company

All those other volunteers, supporters and organisations which have assisted us during the process.

Al-Nisa Associations N.I is grateful to individuals and organisations for their supportive entries for this Book

BCC

Traditionally Belfast is seen as a city with two main communities, a city with two faces. Belfast is changing; the city is now more diverse and may be described as having many faces. As the Equality Officer in the Good Relations Unit at Belfast City Council I am delighted to contribute to this book which recognises that Belfast is changing and acknowledges the continuing hard work of many voluntary and community groups working to involve many different people in our society.

Belfast City Council has been involved with the Muslim community in Northern Ireland for many years. We are delighted to have developed good networks and relationships with many people in the Muslim community.

Since the introduction of Equality Legislation with Section 75 of the Northern Ireland Act in 1998 all Statutory Boards are obliged to ensure that all goods, services and facilities are available to all sections of our society in an equitable way.

Belfast City Council invited Mrs Khan, MBE, Chairperson of Al-Nisa, to contribute to the Equality Video. Her appearance on the video highlights the need for us to be aware of differences in our communities.

In January 2001, the Council adopted a fourth corporate objective, Promoting Good Relations to complement its existing objectives of Providing Civic Leadership, Delivering Best Services and Improving the Quality of Life. The Promoting Good Relations objective integrates and develops our current work in the areas of equality, community relations and cultural diversity and demonstrates our commitment to their underlying principles. Our Corporate Plan states that we 'will encourage and support good relations between all citizens, promoting fair treatment, understanding and respect for people of all cultures'.

The following principles underlie our work:

- To promote equality of opportunity in the discharge of the Councils responsibilities, taking into account the needs of persons of different religious belief, political opinion, racial belief, gender, disability, age, marital status or sexual orientation, and persons with dependants and those without.
- To promote tolerance and understanding throughout the City by providing support, including the equitable use of available budgets, for appropriate initiatives which celebrate the cultural diversity of Belfast City Council
- To promote good relations between people of different religious and political groups beliefs and different racial groups in every aspect of Council activities
- To use the Council's influence as a democratically elected body, providing civic leadership to the City and to promote good relations throughout society

Our vision in terms of this Good Relations Strategy is a stable, tolerant, fair and pluralist society where individuality is respected and diversity is celebrated in an inclusive manner.

We are delighted to have built connections, networks and friendships with Al-Nisa over the last few years. We have met many times to discuss the needs of Muslim Women in our society and we are delighted to help with swimming classes which enable Muslim women to participate. We have had many events at City Hall where the Al-Nisa Association N.I has been invited as key members of our society.

Now more than ever we need to be aware of the needs of the Muslim community in Belfast. We need to make the changes necessary to make Belfast a welcoming city for all traditions, cultures and religions.

We look forward to reading this book and continuing our links with the Al-Nisa Association.

Best Wishes,
Stella Gilmartin

CRC

This publication has received support from the Northern Ireland Community Relations Council which aims to promote a pluralist society characterised by equity, respect for diversity and interdependence. All views expressed in the publication are those of the authors or publisher and should not be understood to be those of the Community Relations Council.

Gender Equality Unit (OFMDFM)

The Office of the First Minister and Deputy First Minister's Gender Equality Unit values the contribution of Al-Nisa Association N.I to the development of its gender equality strategy "Gender Matters" and its action plan.

In consulting with Al-Nisa and other groups, the Gender Equality Unit offered a forum for groups and individuals to express their views and aimed to increase and build the capacity and knowledge of voluntary and community organisations of how policy can be influenced, thereby enabling them to better contribute.

By producing this book, which highlights and shares the positive achievements and contributions Muslims have made in Northern Ireland's society, Al-Nisa is contributing positively to good race and community relations here by addressing some of the misinformation and prejudice with which minority ethnic groups are met.

A coordinated approach by all of society in Northern Ireland to dispel all forms of intolerance is crucial and the group has given us a useful insight into the issues facing Muslim women living in Northern Ireland.
This information has reinforced our commitment to promote equality for all women in Northern Ireland and increase the resolve to work with women of all identities, to enhance the mainstreaming of the gender perspective into all Government policies.

We look forward to maintaining our relationship with Al-Nisa in the future.

Best wishes
Dorina Edgar, Gender Equality Unit, OFMDFM

NICEM

The Al-Nisa Association N.I has been a member organisation of NICEM for the past 6 years. NICEM has supported the organisation through our Capacity Building programme and has seen the organisation grow extensively over those years securing funding for premises, programmes and equipment which have allowed Al-Nisa to diversify their services. At the core of the organisation is the principle of volunteering which NICEM feels is essential to the effective management of all voluntary sector organisations, and Al-Nisa has always believed that it is their commitment as volunteers, although under a lot of pressure, that keeps their organisation strong.

The support which Al-Nisa provides to Muslim women in Northern Ireland through language classes, IT classes, social events and activities and practical advice and support to women in difficulties, is an invaluable service to the community and a testament to hard work by their volunteers.

The group not only works with Muslim women but also works regularly with other minority ethnic groups, voluntary sector and public sector agencies, to raise and address the issues which they feel are important for their members and have participated in many of the public policy consultation activities of NICEM over the last number of years. Issues for the members of Al-Nisa are both issues for the black and minority ethnic sector, but also the women's sector and Al-Nisa has worked together with organisations such as Women's Aid and the Women's Support Network to provide support services for their members and we hope they continue to do so.

This book will introduce the lives, experiences and achievements of many members of the Muslim community to the wider community and highlight the key roles they play in Northern Ireland and how their past and continuing contribution will contribute to a healthy, diverse future.

Gabrielle Doherty

The Northern Ireland Inter-Faith Forum

Any publication which purports to encourage understanding of the growing cultural diversity of Northern Irish society is to be welcomed. In conveying something of the richness and relevance of the Islamic presence within our community, this book promises to be a particularly valuable source of information and enlightenment about what is by far the largest religious minority in Ireland both north and south. In view of the ever present threat and actual incidence of religious and racial intimidation and violence in our land, it is vitally important that the claims and contributions of our Muslim neighbours be understood and acknowledged as a positive and vibrant part of the communal life of our people. This publication is a timely testament to those claims and contributions.

Rev. Maurice Ryan, President of The Northern Ireland Inter-Faith Forum.

QUB

This publication by the Al-Nisa Association of N.I is very much welcomed. It documents the valuable and unique contribution of Muslims to Northern Ireland society and their integration into an increasingly multicultural Northern Ireland. As such it is an important educational source of information about the different cultural backgrounds of the Muslim community. It is also an important and timely resource for increasing our understanding of Islam.
I would like to congratulate the Al-Nisa Association N.I on this publication and wish them continued success in the future.

Dr Mairead Corrigan, Lecturer in Medical Education, QUB.

Stranmillis University College

Awareness and understanding of world religions and inter-faith issues forms an important part of the Religious Studies teaching programme at Stranmillis University College, and learning about Islam is a key element in this process. Such experience is particularly important for student teachers who will be facing increasingly diverse classrooms in the future, both religiously and culturally. As a "non-denominational" academic institution, the task of promoting respect for diversity and of challenging ignorance and prejudice is one in which we are happy to join with people of goodwill in all faiths and communities.

Our teaching and research programmes have been enriched in the past through our various contacts with members of the Muslim community and by the opportunities for visits to Mosques in both parts of Ireland and further afield. We are delighted to welcome this new publication of Al-Nisa as an important contribution to the process of providing clear and accurate insight into Islam and its place in Northern Ireland and we look forward to further enriching opportunities for encounter and exchange.

Norman Richardson
Senior Lecturer in Religious Studies at Stranmillis University College

VSB

VSB is delighted to continue working with the Al-Nisa Association N.I in a variety of roles – as a funder, through the Community Volunteering Scheme Grant, as a recipient of training and as a volunteer placement provider.

Al-Nisa have pro-actively participated in a range of VSB activities including the VOLT (Volunteer Organisations Linking Together) Forums and a "Good Relations" Seminar. A young girl from Al-Nisa has been profiled in the Young Citizens in Action magazine "Action" about her life in Northern Ireland.

The organisation play a most important role in raising awareness and in some cases, de-mystifying the Islamic and Muslim cultures through an interesting and informative delivery.

This book will make an excellent contribution to the positive work carried out within our society by many Muslim people of all ages within Northern Ireland.

Julie Cusick, Corporate Affairs Co-ordinator VSB

WOMEN'S SUPPORT NETWORK

The Women's Support Network would like to congratulate the Al-Nisa Association N.I on the dedicated hard work that the organisation has put into the publication of their book 'Muslims in Northern Ireland'. As a member group of the Womens Support Network we are delighted to support this achievement and look forward to attending the launch of the book at Parliament Buildings, Stormont on the 28th September.

Patricia Haren
Director

Rabia & Ilyas

Al-Nisa is a unique organisation for Muslim women in Northern Ireland.
We have supported the organisation since its inception in Northern Ireland. Al-Nisa has positively contributed to bringing Muslim women together in a united manner and strived to place them at the forefront of the Islamic & non Islamic community.

We from the republic of Ireland will continue to support Al-Nisa and wish the organisation every success in the future.

Rabia & Ilyas,
Dundalk
Republic of Ireland

Historical Journey around the lives of Muslims in Ireland
Dr. Mazhar M. Khan

"Though it is from the East that the Sun rises, showing itself bold and bright, without a veil, it burns and blazes with inward fire only when it escapes from the shackles of East and West.

Drunk with the splendour it springs up out of its East that it may subject all horizon to its mastery, its nature is innocent of both East and West though in origin, true, it is an Easterner". (Mohammad IQBAL, in *Javed Nama*)

Introduction

The study of history is very important for individuals and nations and for a bright future; one should never overlook history. The life of every nation and individuals as a collective body moves in time and passes through, rises and falls, the successes and reverses. Every living nation learns lessons from the people that have lived in the past in order to remember periods of decline and glory [1]. Today's Muslim community in Ireland/ Northern Ireland is not a new phenomenon. There is a large and growing Muslim community in Ireland including Northern Ireland and according to Dr. Comerford there are perhaps more Muslims in Ireland than Methodists [2]. Britain and Ireland have had contact with the Muslim world from its earliest days and there has thus been mutual influence ever since. It is distinctly possible that Muslims arrived in Ireland as long ago as the year 845 (A.D.) when al-Ghazali was sent by Abdul Rehman II, ruler of Cordova on a diplomatic mission to the Vikings [2].

As with Christianity the first Muslim came to the South of Ireland. It is said that great St. Declan might have been the first to baptise a Christian in the South of Ireland in 402 AD, some 30 years before St. Patrick. This occurred around Ardmore and Youghall, in south of Ireland near Cork [3]. The Ballycottin Cross (900 A.D.), possibly an ecclesiastical artefact, was found at Ballycottin on the southern coast of Ireland. Its contents are peculiar and like King Offa's coin it also bears an Arabic inscription. At the centre of this four armed bronze cross, set in a glass head in the Kufic Arabic script, is the phrase **Bismillah** ("In the name of Allah) [4]. This cross is now kept in the British Museum. It is one of many artefacts found from this period indicating a strong link with Muslim civilisation and is further evidence of Islam's interaction with Britain and Ireland in that period.

13

In addition to these accounts of Muslims coming to Ireland before the 15th century, there are indirect indications that some Muslims might have come to Ireland in the 14th and 15th centuries during the Moorish reign of Spain most likely to the south of Ireland. Nasrid Moorish rulers sent emissaries to Western Europe including England and possibly Ireland (Plate 1). Some places in the South of Ireland particularly around Cork have names which have meanings similar in the Arabic language [5]. The Corsairs from North Africa, the Ottomans and the last Moorish rulers in Spain did have some contact with Western Europe and also there is an account of sea excursions to Southern England and to Southern Ireland by Algerian Corsairs. They raided the south coast of Ireland regularly and among those they captured was the brother of the Bishop of Waterford and Lismore, Rev. Comerford [2]. The first documented contact of a North African/descendents of the Marinides and Ottoman rulers of Algeria occurred in June 1631 in the form of Algerian naval ships, off the Mizen Head in the South of Ireland. Two naval ships sailed to the harbour through Bantry Bay and occupied Baltimore, [6-9]. They remained there for some time. This prompted the poet Thomas Davies (1804-1845) to write of the event in his ballad – "The Yell of Allah breaks above the Prayers, the shriek, the roar. Oh! Blessed God, the Algerine is Lord of Baltimore"[2,6]. This was partly on account of the events which were happening in Cork at that time. Sir William Hull who owned most of the land and fishery rights had major conflict with the local people. They were unhappy about the levy for fishing rights. There was thus a great deal of upheaval as well as a rebellion against English rule. The English officer Captain Cole had burnt Crosshaven, Leamcon and Schull belonging to Sir William Hull. He was attacked by both sides in the Rebellion of 1641 and suffered great losses. . He was friendly with a Dutch shipman, Claus Campion, who used his base in the south west of Cork and waylaid several ships, especially the great East Indiamen[6]. It is said that he might have captured over a hundred ships in that period and the booty from those ships was taken to the small republic of Sallee on the North African coast or to Leamcon in Co. Cork, thus bringing trade and merchants from North Africa to this area. The trading links were continued despite the retreat of Algerian ships from Baltimore [9].

Cork was becoming a major trading centre – elephant tusks, tobacco, spices, wool, leather, precious stones and metals were regularly brought in from Asia and North Africa and traded there. Trade was also the lifeblood of Muslim civilization and Muslim countries were the source of many items sought by the Europeans.

PLATE I

Abdullah el-Duahed ben –Massoud:
A 15th century Moorish Ambassador to England

A new world had opened up for Europe following Columbus's expedition to America and Vasco da Gamma's to India in the 1490s. Britain took a keen interest in foreign trade and companies like Levant and East India were founded to promote trade and influence in the Mediterranean and South East Asian countries, most of them ruled by Muslims. These companies later acquired such power as to change the course of history of the world. The opening of Suez in 1869 heralded the recruitment of scores of seamen known as Lascars from Yemen, North Africa and India [10]. Many of those settled in and around major seaports. Some Europeans who travelled and lived in Muslim lands also converted to Islam.

Story of Sake Dean Mahomet

One of the earliest documented arrivals of an Indian Muslim in Ireland was that of a man called Sake (Sheikh) Dean Mahomet (Plate II). Dean Mahomet was born in 1759 (or earlier as per his own account later) in Patna (Bihar), India [10-13], which is situated a few hundred miles to the north of Calcutta. It was the headquarters of the British East India Company at that time. Dean Mahomet's family came from a military background and he himself entered into the military service of the British East India Army. He joined The East India (British) army as a footman to an officer; the officer in question was Godfrey Evan Baker of the East India regiment. Baker's father was well known and an established businessman in Cork. Baker himself became a Captain in 1781. Dean Mahomet also rose to the rank of a Subedar (subaltern lieutenant). Both Baker and Dean Mahomet later moved to Cork in 1784 when Baker resigned his Commission. Baker then married into a very influential family in Cork and it appears that Dean Mahomet was looked after by this family after the death of Captain Baker in 1786. In Cork, Mahomet went to college to improve his English and he married a lady, Jane Daly. In 1794 he published his first book called the "Travels of Dean Mahomet". Only a few copies now exist. It was printed in two volumes. A complete set of both volumes is available in the India Office Library, National Library of Ireland and the Catholic Ursuline Convent. Only one volume remains in the library of the University of Cork. It has now been republished along with a biographical essay from Michael Fisher of Oberlin College, Ohio [12]. This republication and the biographical essay is of enormous help to the students of history in understanding the complexities of Dean Mahomet's personality and the struggle he had to endure in order to assimilate in the society of Cork, yet maintain his own individuality.

PLATE 2

Sake Dean Mahomet.
(Courtesy Brighton Museum and Art Gallery)

The writing and ultimate publication of the book by Dean Mahomet was a remarkable undertaking especially from a man with a modest educational background and knowledge of English until his arrival in Ireland. His book was subscribed by many influential persons in the Cork Society and a good number of them had contacts with India. It was meant to be a guide for the Irishman who would be seeking employment through the East India Company in India. He dedicated this book to Colonel William A Bailey of Co. Down who also served in India. The book was in the form of letters and it is in two volumes. It essentially deals with many aspects of life and travel in India, in addition to his own experience in the British East India Army. The book was extremely well written and although Dean Mahomet started to improve his English while in Cork it appears that he had mastered the language very well. He chose the fashionable English genre for the narrative of his travels. It contains letters addressed to a fictional European friend enabling him to establish a personal relationship with British/Irish readers of that era [12].

Mirza Abu Talib

In 1799 Mahomet met another Muslim from India by the name of **Mirza Abu Talib Khan**. His ship was prevented from landing in England due to stormy seas. It took shelter in the Cove of Cork at the end of a very difficult journey due to adverse winds. Abu Talib khan was well connected and was invited to come to England by Captain Richardson of British East India Army. Abu Talib was referred to by him as a "Persian Prince. Abu Talib also knew Marquis Cornwallis formerly Governor General of India (1786-1793) then Lord Lieutenant of Ireland (1798-1801) and later Governor General of India again in 1805. While dining in Cork he met Captain Massey Baker whom he recognised from his days in India. Baker invited him to his estate of Fortwilliam outside of the town of Cork and introduced him to Dean Mahomet. After his triumphant stay in Ireland and England enjoying the hospitality of the high society, he returned to India. He described his travels and stay in his book which was published in 1810 (MaAsir-e Talibi) [14]. The book was written in Persian. Mirza Abu Talib came from Muslim Service elite and was well placed among the ruling and literary elite in India. He was probably related to the then Persian Ambassador in Britain, Mirza Abul Hassan Khan (Plate 3)[15]. In this book, Mirza Abu Talib Khan described Dean Mahomet as follows.

"Mention of a Muslim named Dean Mahomet: Another person in the house of the aforementioned Captain (William Massey Baker) is named Dean Mahomet.

PLATE 3

Mirza Abul Hassan Khan,
Persian Ambassador to England in early 19th century

He is from Murshidabab (formerly capital of Muslim Bengal). A brother of Captain Baker raised him from childhood as a member of the family. He brought him to Cork and sent him to school where he learnt to read and write English well. Dean Mahomet, after completing his studies, ran off to another city with a fair and beautiful daughter of a family of status in Cork who was studying with him. He then married her and had several beautiful children with her. He has a separate house and wealth. He also wrote a book about his travels and account of himself and customs of India"[14,16].

Mirza Abu Talib khan was well connected and came from a very respectable family. It is not clear what his occupation was, but was clearly well off financially. He travelled extensively in England and Ireland.

Dean Mahomed (Mahomet) in England

After spending over 20 years in Ireland, Mahomet moved to England most likely around 1805. There might have been several reasons including the bloody Rebellion in 1798, and his reported incompatibility with Mrs Baker (Mrs Massey Baker), but the Act of Union in 1801 was perhaps the turning point for these early arrivals in Ireland to move to England for better financial prospects. After his arrival In London, he worked for the Earl of Dundonald, Hon. Basil Cochrane, promoting exotic oriental therapies. He also opened a café –Hindustan Coffee House. He later settled in Brighton and introduced Oriental medicinal vapour baths and therapeutic massage. They were quite popular in Cork and so Mahomet's establishment also became quite well known in Brighton for the steaming baths which were used for all sorts of ailments. Brighton was a fashionable health resort in those days and sea bathing for rheumatic ailments was popular and Brighton was not very far from London. The rich and famous flocked to him and his clients included the Prime minister, Sir Robert Peel, and King George IV appointed him as his personal shampooing surgeon. In the last 40 years of his life, in the seaside resort of Brighton, he rose to popular fame as a Shampooing surgeon, specialising in his own invention of medicinal Vapour bath and by Royal appointment to King George IV and King William IV. The shampooing in those days meant far more than washing hair. It involved steaming, aromatic baths or even vigorous massage and was mostly of a medicinal nature [10-13].

His travels and life reveal much about the diverse roles taken by Indians, especially Muslims within the British Empire in India and Ireland. Once he moved to Brighton, he changed the spelling of his name to Mohamed which is closer to the classical spelling rather than the previous one of "Mahomet" (as used by Voltaire).

In 1820 and 1822 Mahomet published two further books entitled "Cases cured by Sake Dean Mahomed" and "Shampooing – the benefits resulting from the use of Indian medicated vapour bath". Mahomed died in 1851 in Brighton [12].

Dean Mohamed, during his life span, passed through many worlds; India as it came under British rule, Ireland as an English colony and later on England as it became an imperial power [12]. In each of these worlds Dean Mahomet crossed cultural boundaries, while living, writing, marrying and raising a family in Ireland in the 18th century. Dean Mahomet came across in the words of Edward Said, "hybrid, historical and cultural experiences and how they crossed national boundaries" [17].

Over his nearly 20 years of residency in Ireland, despite the bitter struggle of diverse groups about Irish national identity and the relationship to the direct British rule, he found a place for himself, distinct both from the local Catholic population and the ruling Protestant Irish. An interesting portrayal of his image in Ireland is derived not only from his own book of 'travels of Dean Mahomet' but also from a contemporary account of Mirza Abu Talib Khan who toured Ireland and England from 1799 to 1803 (Travels of Mirza – Translated by Charles Stewart; 1810) [16].

Despite the unquestionable authorship of his travels, many Westerners of his day believed that Asians were incapable of authoring such an eminently polished work of English literature interspersed with Latin quotes. Unlike other British contemporary writers, Dean Mohamed's book presented Indians as human beings worthy of respect. They had weaknesses and virtues, different and possibly superior in some ways to those of European. Although Dean Mahomed wrote for the British (Anglo Irish) elite on whom he had to depend for publishing his epistolary account, yet he stressed the virtues and flaws of both British and Indian cultures, each of which made an enormous impact to shape his identity [12]. His book remains an important counter argument to any partisan view of English literature during the age of Imperialism as the sole preserve of Europeans [17].

Other Muslims in 17th and 18th century in Ireland

While detailing Mr. Dean Mahomet's achievements and his contribution towards literature and Oriental Medicine, we tend to overlook the contribution of another Irish Muslim called **Dr. Achmet** (1728-1797)[18&19]. He was of Irish/Turkish descent and was a renowned Physician practicing in Dublin. He espoused the virtues of the medicinal bath. He promoted and published papers in 1772, nearly forty years before Dean Mohamed established his own version of medicinal baths. He presented his research findings and recommendations to a committee of the whole Faculty of Physicians and Surgeons (Later Royal College of Physicians and Surgeons). He thus remains a potential subject of further research on Irish Muslims and their contribution in eighteenth century[18].

Alexander Cobb (1788-1836) married **Nazir Begum**, daughter of **Aziz Jehan** [10], a Mughal princess from Kashmir. He collected object d'art from India which included Indian and Mughal paintings, miniatures and other manuscripts, which were exhibited at the Newbridge House Museum, County Dublin on his return to Ireland in 1828. It is not clear what happened to Nazir Begum after the death of Alexander Cobb in 1836.

Mirza Itesa Moodin arrived in England in 1775. According to his observation, English had never seen a 'Munshi' (a senior official) dressed in Jamah (Long coat), turban, sash and dagger. Being familiar with poor wandering Lascars, they took him to be a Prince or Nabob (Nawab) [10]. Scores of people visited him, some out of curiosity and others with genuine cordiality. He was invited to Ireland by Lord Cornwallis who knew him well. He was deeply impressed by London and thought that it was the most beautiful city.

Munshi Mohammad Ismail (1772) and **Mir Mohammad Husain** also visited Britain, but the most revealing was the account of **Mirza Abu Talib Khan** about England and Ireland. He was not only complementary about the customs but was also critical of certain aspects [14-16].

Islam and Great Britain/Ireland from the 19th Century

The positive aspects, the social and cultural gain which Europe has acquired through its contact with Muslims, are often overshadowed by conflict, tension and rivalry. There is a tradition of deep and long historical and contemporary engagement between Islam and the West. Culture and knowledge have moved both ways from Europe to Near East as had the conquest and so has the religion especially the three main written have pushed west ward and east ward. Transmission of knowledge from Near East to Europe occurred primarily through Islamic presence [23]. But there was a great deal of contact that did not involve conquest or any kind of military struggle. Similarly trade expanded rapidly to Europe mainly through the Mediterranean after the Eleventh century [8&9, 23].

Although Islam is one of the major religions being practiced by approximately one fifth of the world population, it remains to many people an unknown quantity [20-22]. In the UK there are substantial Muslim communities (nearly two million), yet Islam is often misunderstood and misrepresented. Islam is an Arabic word and connotes submission, surrender and obedience. As a religion, Islam stands for complete submission and obedience to God Almighty and that is why it is called Islam. The other literary meaning of the word Islam is peace and this signifies that one can achieve real peace of body and of mind only through submission and obedience to God. Such a life of obedience brings in peace of the heart and establishes a real peace in society at large [21].

Industrial and economic expansion has brought renewed prosperity to Europe in the middle of the last century, bringing large numbers of immigrants including Muslims to Britain. Coming for the most part from the Indian sub-continent and speaking different languages, these people found employment in a variety of occupations. Today the Muslim community, estimated at around two million, comprises a wide spectrum of immigrant experience, ranging from those who are struggling to survive in their new found environment and to those who have considerable prosperity, wealth and influence. Many have achieved distinction in their field and some have been suitably honoured [22].

Muslims in 20th Century Ireland

The recent arrival of Muslims in large numbers to the island of Ireland began after the Second World War although some arrived immediately after the First World War. There are nearly six thousand Muslims in the Republic of Ireland including many students. Similarly, in Northern Ireland Muslims are the third largest religious group. Ireland had a very close connection with many parts of the world which inhabited Muslims in significantly large numbers, namely, North

Africa, the Middle East and the Indian Sub-Continent. Several well-known persons played a very significant role in the Indian Sub-Continent – Lord and Lady Dufferin from Co. Down for example. Lord Dufferin was Governor General of India and Lady Dufferin was known for her social welfare work; at least 2 large hospitals were named after her. Lord John Lawrence of Londonderry was Governor of Punjab [24]. The famous Lawrence Gardens was named after him and is now called Bagh-e-Jinah after the founder of Pakistan, Mohammad Ali Jinah. Similarly many hospital and other institutions were named after Ulster people like Lady Irwin, wife of Lord Irwin (Governor of Punjab) had a Women's hospital in Lahore named after her.

Muslims in Ireland, like the vast majority of fellow Muslims are peaceable, law abiding and eminently charitable in their outlook [22]. It would be a grave error of judgment to lump them together in any generalised and judgmental way. The rich religious tradition that Islam represents is unique by its unity on major principles and diversity in traditions. Globally speaking it is followed by one fifth of the world's population. The present Muslim community in Northern Ireland comprises of descendents of those who arrived between the two world wars and those who arrived within the last few decades. In the early 1960's there were about 100 Muslims in the North. Today's Northern Ireland community numbers are around three to four thousand, mainly from the Indian subcontinent, but also many nationalities including some from the Middle East, Malaysia, North Africa and some from Northern Ireland.

Muslims in the Irish Republic

The recent history goes back to 1950, when only a few of Muslims were living in Irish Republic. This mainly consisted of the Muslim students who came to Ireland for further studies. In 1959 the Dublin Islamic Society was formed mostly by students. This Society was registered as a friendly society and acquired charitable status in 1971 and later became the current Islamic Foundation of Ireland. The first Mosque in Ireland was established in Dublin in 1975 at Herrington Street, Dublin 8. In order to meet the growing needs of the community the present Mosque and an Islamic centre was established in 1983 in South Circular Road

DUBLIN ISLAMIC CENTRE PROJECT

Muslim students started to arrive in Eire after the Second World War. In 1950 the number of students from South Africa, North Africa, Pakistan and India were increasing. A large number of them were studying medicine but some also enrolled to study English and Science.

The majority chose to live in the Rathmines, Harrington Street, Leeson Street and South Circular Road areas. At that time few Irish Christians living in Dublin converted to Islam. The first Irish man to become a Muslim was a Patrick Conway who renamed himself Mohammad Conway. The second name in the list was a Mr. Gerry Adam, renaming himself as Abdullah Adam.

The first Islamic Society in Ireland was established in 1959. It was formed by the Muslim students and was called the **Dublin Islamic Society** (later called the **Islamic Foundation of Ireland**). At that time there was no Mosque in Dublin. Formal prayers were conducted in private houses/flats. The students' houses and some rented halls were used for Jum'ah (Friday) and Eid prayers. In 1969 the students began to contact their relatives, some Islamic organizations and Muslim countries for the purpose of collecting donations to establish a Mosque. In 1976 the first Mosque and Islamic Centre in Ireland was opened in a four storey building at No. 7, Harrington Street, Dublin 8. Among those who contributed to the project of the Mosque and Islamic Centre was the late King Faisal bin Abdul Aziz Saudi of Arabia. The establishment of the Dublin Islamic Society /Islamic foundation of Ireland in chronological order and minutes of the meeting are stated in appendix I.

Important dates in the establishment of Islamic societies in Ireland outside Dublin include:

1978.   The Galway Islamic Society (in the west of Ireland) was established, and a house was rented to be used for the Friday and congregational prayers in the city

1981.   A house was bought in Galway to be used as a Mosque for the Muslims in the City.

1984.   The Cork Muslim Society (in the South of Ireland) was established. Cork is the second largest city in Ireland after Dublin. A house was rented for the Muslims to perform their prayers.

1986.   The Ballyhaunis Mosque in the Northwest of Ireland was built.

1990.   The Muslim National School in Dublin was opened. It is the first Muslim school recognized and funded by the Irish Department of Education.

1994.   A house was bought in the city of Cork to be used as a Mosque for the Muslims in the City.

1994.   A house was bought in Limerick in the Mid-South of Ireland to be used as a Mosque for the Muslims in the City.

1996.   The Islamic Cultural Centre was opened in Dublin following a generous donation by Sheikh Hamdan bin Rashid Al-Maktoum, Deputy Governor of Dubai and Minister of Finance and Industry in the United Arab Emirates. It consists of a purpose built beautiful mosque and a School.

1999.   A branch of the Islamic Foundation of Ireland in the City of Waterford was formed. A house was rented for the prayers and classes for adults and children were commenced.

Muslims in Northern Ireland

The history of Muslims, their arrival in Northern Ireland and their contributions towards the Northern Ireland society can be divided into two phases. The first phase consists of the period after the First World War, up to 1960. This was mostly a time for hard work ethic fuelled by the desire to better oneself, business enterprise, entrepreneurship and establishing a root in Northern Ireland society. Several people, after a small beginning, prospered to hold successful businesses, mainly in the clothing trade or in the food trade.

Some Muslims came with Maharaja Ranjitsingh, Jamsahab of Nawanagar as members of his staff. The Maharaja bought Ballynahinch Castle in Connemara. One of his staff was a Mr. Khan, who married an Irish lady and later lived in Dungannon and then in Cookstown. Although he was a cook, he later started door to door selling clothes and other utilities. He was very hard working. He had a friend, Ghulam Mohammad also known as Shah Mohammad who also lived nearby in Castledawson. He was the brother of Nathoo Mohammad of Glasgow, one of the first shop keepers and itinerant trader in the United Kingdom. The other recorded person to arrive in Northern Ireland in 1920 was a Mr. Ali. He came from Cuba. He was working there as a bonded labourer in a sugar cane farm. He jumped a ship which had anchored at Liverpool. He was advised to go to the South of Ireland as it was about to become a republic and the chance of him being caught by immigration officials was slim. He arrived in

Northern Ireland and met Mr. Khan who was already settled here. He lived in Castlecaulfield near Dungannon. At the same time, two Ali brothers also lived in Northern Ireland, around Dungannon. One of them was called Mohammad Ali. They were from a small village in Faisalabad (now Pakistan). Mohammad Ali died in early fifties. His grand nephew currently lives in Belfast with his family. There is some confusion about the identities of these two people named Ali from Cuba and Pakistan [25]. Actually both came from Punjab, Pakistan. None of them were deported. Several other Muslims arrived from North Africa and Yemen after the First World War but never stayed here for any length of time. They moved to Bristol, Cardiff and Glasgow.

A Gentleman by the name of Lal Khan of Mirpur (Azad Kashmir) also arrived in 1924. He apparently knew Mr. Ali of Cuba and also knew Ghulam Mohammad of Castledawson. He started door to door sales of clothing and tailoring. Lal Khan was an illiterate person and could not read or write English or Urdu. He married a local lady. He was a very hard working man. His wife, Mary was very good with book- keeping and helped him with his business. Lal Khan however had an amazing memory of all his clients' requirements, their sizes of clothes and their other orders. She would however write down the details of his business at the end of each day and then would accompany him to visit his customers every month to check the accounts. He had many children. He was very generous and regularly supported his other members of his family including his brothers, sisters and his mother in his native village in Pakistan. He died in 1974. He wished to be buried according to Islamic customs. Unfortunately his grave had to be readjusted for him to face Mecca upon his death. Mr Lal Khan's story is very well narrated by Kapoor in his book 'The Irish Raj' [26].

Most of the Asians at that time were involved in the clothing itinerant trade often referred to as peddling or 'door business'. This itinerant trade though required very hard work and was quite popular amongst the people from the Indian subcontinent including Hindus, Sikhs and Muslims. Most traders started their business in this fashion and later were successful enough to acquire large businesses. Their customers, coming from urban housing schemes and rural village communities, were mostly from the poor working class and paid with weekly instalments. Northern Ireland was ideal for this type of trade because of its widely scattered communities in rural and suburban areas. One important reason why itinerant door to door traders were able to continue was that they offered interest free credit at a price which compared very favourably with regular shops. Another factor was their willingness to reach out to remote areas where shops were few and far between and few people had their own transport. In many cases they provided personal services by offering alterations and fitted garments to their clients, thus bringing the custom to their door steps. This inevitably resulted in jealousy and accusations that the goods sold by peddlers were of inferior quality. Actually the goods acquired by the regular shop keepers were often from the same source but there was substantial overhead cost. In war time Ireland, some Dublin wholesalers threatened to remove their patronage from W.B. McCarter's factory, Fruit of the Loom, if he continued to supply textiles to the successful retailers from Indian subcontinent, but McCarter, however refused to be bullied [10,27].

These early itinerant traders did not experience any racism overtly or otherwise from the host community at that time. In fact their experience was quite positive as they were often helped in their trade. Some even learned to drive with the help of locals. This was perhaps another reason for their continued stay and success in Northern Ireland. A letter sent by Lal Khan to his relatives in his native village mentioned how he found local people to be very friendly and helpful. This information was a definite stimulus for others to come to Northern Ireland despite the sectarian divide. Many early settlers were completely oblivious of this religious conflict. The story that a Muslim, while out walking, was menacingly questioned to reveal if he was a catholic Muslim or a Protestant Muslim, is often narrated at after dinner speeches. There is no authentic account of it ever happening.

The next group of Muslims arrived in 1930-45 and later established themselves with very successful business ventures in Northern Ireland. One of them was Ghulam Mohammad affectionately called 'Boss'. He started as a door to door salesman but soon established himself as a successful manufacturer of clothing, owning his factory in Belfast (plate 4). At the peak of his business, in the early Sixties, he employed over 15 people. He was the President of the first Pakistan Society in Belfast and was thus invited to meet Late F.M. Ayub Khan, then President of Pakistan who was visiting Britain. His daughter and nephew live in Belfast. He was a very generous person, always willing to help. He started in partnership with another successful business person, the late Mr. Nizam Dean.

Mr. Dean opened a factory in 1946 in the Old Park area of Belfast. Mr. Dean came from Faisalabad (Pakistan) and arrived in Belfast in 1932. He had to endure a very tough life during his early years as a door to door salesman, carrying a

PLATE 4

Mr. Ghulam Mohammad 'Boss',
One of the first Muslim itinerant traders to come to Northern Ireland
and set up a clothing business.

suitcase full of clothes around on a bicycle or on foot, in all sorts of weather. He was very hard working and had a very impressive personality. His outward appearance marked by impeccable sartorial style always made a very favourable impression on his customers and belied his illiteracy, although he was able to converse freely in English. His secretary of fifteen years remained unaware that he could not read or write English. He would ask her to read the correspondences and dictate the replies. He was often seen carrying a Times daily newspaper [28]. He was a brilliant businessman and his factory in Belfast employed as many as 70- 80 workers. This was the first factory owned by a person from the Indian Sub-continent in Belfast. He was also invited to meet the President of Pakistan, Ayub Khan during his visit to Britain in 1966 (Plate 5). Mr Nizam Dean's younger brother, the late Mr. Jamal Dean, after a modest beginning, also became a very successful businessman in Belfast. He also owned a knitwear factory. His two sons and grand children currently live in Belfast.

Mr. Shah Dean arrived in Northern Ireland in 1956. After a modest start with a small business and sheer hard work, he became a very successful businessman. He acquired a large clothing warehouse in Donegall Street in the centre of Belfast (plate 6). He was elected as treasurer of the first Pakistani Association in Belfast in 1961. His house in north Belfast was the meeting point for the Pakistani and Muslim community in Belfast in 1960s. He was elected as Vice President of the first standing committee in 1976. A building was purchased as premises for The Belfast Islamic Centre in 1980. This was insufficient for the needs of growing Muslim population. The present location of Belfast Islamic Centre is at 38 Wellington Park. It was acquired in 1986.

Shah Dean later became the Trustee of the Belfast Islamic Centre. He remained trustee of the Centre for the next 17 years and retired from trusteeship in 1997. He was a very generous man and was of considerable financial help for the acquisition of the current Islamic Centre with an interest free loan. His son Haji Mohammad Lateef is currently one of the Trustees of Belfast Islamic Centre.

Muslims and sectarian Conflict in Northern Ireland

The vast majority of Muslims who settled here during the days of "Troubles" remained unaffected. They had never taken side in the conflict between the two communities in Northern Ireland. In most cases their work as businessmen or as professionals was not affected, but it was impossible to escape the effects of the "Troubles" completely. A Muslim from Pakistan, named Nauroz Khan was murdered on 26th June 1973 while working as a civilian lorry driver for the

PLATE 5

Mr. Nizam Dean, (second from left), with President of Pakistan, FM Ayub Khan during his visit to Britain in November 1966. Mr. Ghulam Mohammad 'Boss' with white cap is second from right. Mr. Nizam Dean was the first person from the Indian subcontinent to set up a factory in Northern Ireland.

Army. Another worker called Mohammad Khan aged eighteen was killed while working as a tea boy in an army barracks. These were isolated incidents and the Muslim community did not suffer any major upheaval. Very few Muslims left Northern Ireland as a direct result of being affected by the conflict. Some Muslims left Northern Ireland purely for business, professional or family reasons.

Muslims in Academia

Muslims made a significant contribution towards academic life in the Universities in Northern Ireland and gained a well earned reputation in their fields. Dr. Omar Farouki, a senior lecturer in Civil Engineering at Queens University, Mr Quamer Hossain, Senior Lecturer in Electrical Engineering, Mrs Mary Hossain, senior Lecturer in French at Queens University and Dr Mustafa Akai at the University of Ulster are just a few to be mentioned.

Current Era

During the next era saw the arrival of technocrats, students and doctors – mostly for postgraduate training. Several of them stayed after gaining higher qualifications. They obtained employment in the Universities and in industry namely **Dr. Raza**, **Dr. Yusuf**, **Mr. Ahmad Shareef**, **Mr Hossain** and **Dr. Farouki**. The account of their contributions and achievements are mentioned in the next chapter. This was also the period when Muslims decided to have a permanent place for congregational prayers and other religious functions. This period also coincided with the arrival of many junior doctors for higher medical training. They later found jobs in the health services attaining important positions. **Dr. A. Majeed Siddiqui** of Londonderry, a psychiatrist, was honorary secretary of the BMA of the North Western Division and held many other important positions in the Overseas Doctors Association including its founder President and the Chairman. He was also President of Belfast Islamic Centre from 1978-80 and later a Trustee from 1980 to 1990 Many Muslim doctors contributed significantly in the field of medicine, becoming consultants in the teaching hospitals. The most well known is **Dr. Harith Lamki**, originally from Oman and a graduate of Trinity College Dublin. During his student days he was a member of the first committee to form the Islamic Society of Dublin. He is a well-known consultant gynaecologist. He was a postgraduate advisor to the Royal College of Obstetrics and Gynaecology and an undergraduate and postgraduate examiner not only in the United Kingdom

PLATE 6

Mr. Shah Dean arrived in Northern Ireland in 1956.
He was one of the first Trustees of the Belfast Islamic Centre.

but also for other universities abroad.

Establishment of the Belfast Islamic Centre

Islam is the religion of unity based on the belief on oneness of God Almighty. Islam requires that Muslims should perform the prayers in association with other Muslims, preferably at a Mosque or a place of congregation. It is therefore important for Muslims to offer prayers congregationally and not ignore it. This practice enhances the spirit of community. The first priority for Muslims in a foreign or non-Muslim society is thus to establish a place to pray in congregation.

There are many similarities between the establishment of the Belfast Islamic Centre/mosque and the Dublin Islamic society. Both communities had to struggle hard to acquire a place of worship and congregational prayers. The main difference is that the impetus to establish a Centre/ Mosque in Belfast came equally from students and already settled Muslims mainly in the business community, while in Dublin; it was mainly the students who were the main driving force. In addition the Islamic Culture Centre and Mosque in Dublin was built with a very generous grant from Sheikh Hamdan Bin Rashid Al Makhtoom of Dubai. The efforts to establish a Mosque and Centre here in Northern Ireland were all voluntary and local with virtually no help from outside.

The first meeting to consider the formation of a society to organise regular congregational prayers was held in 1961, mainly by businessmen of Pakistani origin who were well settled in Northern Ireland.

The next serious attempt was made in 1975 by the postgraduate students, university lectures, doctors in training and business men (Plate 7). A standing committee was elected (Appendix III).

The Belfast Islamic Centre acquired premises at Eglantine Ave. in 1980 after sterling efforts by many Muslims, mainly **Mr. Quamer Hossein, Dr. Yusuf Hanore**, the late **A. Ghafoor**, the Late **Mohammad Hanif, Mr. Shah Dean** and the late **Dr. Naseem Akhtar**. Their drive, dedication and commitment were exemplary. The late **Dr. Naseem Akhtar** was a very sincere person. His efforts and contribution to establish a Centre for Muslims in Belfast were enormous. With his premature death, the Muslim community lost a very friendly, pleasant, sincere and conscientious person. He was always

PLATE 7

Participants of the meeting held in 1975 to consider the establishment of Belfast Islamic Centre. Standing are Dr. Yusuf Hanore (far left) and the late Dr. Naseem Akhtar (far right). Mr. Quamer Hossain (elected president) is standing third from right. Mr. Mohammad Bashir and Late Ghulam Mustafa are sitting far left and far right respectively.

remembered for his sense of humour.

Mr. Quamer Hossain, a senior lecturer in the Department of Electrical Engineering in Queens University Belfast was the first President of Belfast Islamic Centre. He and his wife, **Mrs Mary Hossain** are great inspiration for Muslims. Mary Hossain was also a senior lecturer in the French Language at Queens University. Mr. Hossain's knowledge of Islam is vast and he never hesitated in providing advice to young and newly arrived Muslims. He was largely responsible for the establishment of the Islamic Centre and he promoted educational and intellectual interaction. He has a large collection of books not only about Islam but about a wide array of subjects. The Hossains are well known for their intellectual pursuits and enlightened company.

The present premises of the Belfast Islamic Centre were acquired during the days when **Dr. Farouki** was President. It was his dedication and focussed approach which made it possible for the community to acquire the current centre. Fund raising was carried out for this project by many of those already mentioned above. In addition, **Mr. Shah Dean** and the Late **Haji Ghulam Mustafa** very generously supported the establishment of the Belfast Islamic Centre by financial assistance. The Decision to purchase the current premises was to be taken at a General body meeting and to Dr. Farouki's chagrin, it had to be postponed due to the lack of a quorum and reconvened two weeks later to approve the purchase of the house later converted as a Mosque/Centre.

The most noticeable change and progress in the functioning of the Belfast Islamic Centre occurred when **Dr. Mamun Mobayed** was President from 1992-2000. He was president for 8 years giving stability and favourable media exposure to the Belfast Islamic Centre. He was Chairman of the Inter Faith Forum of Northern Ireland. This era experienced the most notable progress in the functioning of the Belfast Islamic Centre. During this period regular contacts were established with the Belfast City Hall and the Belfast Islamic Centre established a tradition to invite the Lord Mayor of Belfast for an annual gathering after the Eid Celebration.

Currently, it is estimated that there are over 3000 -4000 Muslims in Northern Ireland. They originate from over 30 countries. Some of them are students but a substantial proportion who are well established, consider Northern Ireland their home. They contribute significantly towards the progress and prosperity of this part of the world (see next chapter). They are working in different fields including academia, the health provision sector, namely in hospitals and general medical practice, private business and other technical institutions.

In addition to the Belfast Islamic Centre, other organisations like Al-Nisa and Northern Ireland Muslim Family Association (NIMFA) also provide support to Muslim men and women. They all have charitable status and help Muslims to integrate and be involved with constructive work for the betterment of the society at large. Al- Nisa was established to support Muslim women in 1998. It is a totally voluntary organization and is run by Muslim Women and provides a platform for building bridge between Muslim women and the wider community. In addition to providing women with information on human rights, It also provides adult education classes.

Conclusion

We have come a long way from being an isolated Muslim living in a remote area to becoming a strong community, fully involved in the building of the society and development of the community. Islam being a global religion, Muslims spread in all parts of Europe and America. Ireland being no exception, significant numbers came to Ireland as well. However the numbers were not large as compared to England and other parts of the United Kingdom where they made a lasting impression bringing with them a rich and varied culture. The impression has not been as indelible in Northern Ireland as it has occurred in England where there are many associations, organisations and Mosques dotted around the country in addition to many TV channels, Newspapers and other activities. The lack of mainline political activity has also discouraged Muslims from getting involved in local politics. Development and enrichment is a two way process, not only does it affect the Muslims through the mutual influences they encounter but it also affects the community at large towards a better enrichment.

I am grateful to my many friends who have provided me with very helpful information. I am grateful to Al-Nisa for giving me this opportunity to write this monograph. I am also thankful to my wife for her unending energy and enthusiasm firstly as Chairperson of Al-Nisa but for her constant persuasion and encouragement to complete this chapter and secondly, for the multiple printing of the draft and reviewing various versions. As with any monograph of this type, much more is likely to be omitted or missed than included. I had earlier presented a brief paper about the History of Muslims in Ireland and this chapter is a continuation of the previous effort. I intend to further update it later as the subject is new, vast and interesting. Much still remains to be researched and it is hoped that this contribution will stimulate further research in order to advance our knowledge of this important field and little known aspect of Muslim history in Ireland and Irish/British Muslim identity. Any omissions will clearly need to be rectified in future attempts, as the current contribution is by no means exhaustive or complete. I am also grateful to the Brighton History centre and Brighton Museum and Art Gallery, Royal Pavilion Gardens especially to Ms. Donna Steele and Paul Jordan for supplying me with photographs of Dean Mahomet and quotations from him and his grateful patients. I am thankful to Ray Mullan of Community Relations Council who kindly reviewed the manuscript and for his valuable suggestions.

I have benefited immensely from the following books and have borrowed extensively from them, especially the narrative of various accounts. These books are extremely well written and possess a rich documentation of the period that I have attempted to describe in this monograph. Some of these books offer information from obscure sources yet are well researched. There are minor details about the dates and I have presented my own interpretation of dates and events which may be different from those described in them. I therefore take full responsibility for any errors, misprints, omissions and commissions while giving all credit to the authors of the books mentioned below.

The travels of Dean Mohammed: edited with an introduction and biographical essay by Michael Fisher; University of California Press (1996).

Islam in Europe: by Jack Goody (2004) Polite Press/Blackwell Publishing Ltd.
Culture and Imperialism: by Edward Said; New York Press.
The Irish Raj: by Narinder Kapoor; Greystone Press: Northern Ireland.
Ireland from the Sea: by Andrew Phelan (1998); Wolfhound Press.
Asians in Britain: 400 years of history: by Rozina Visram (2002), Pluto Press.
Urdu and Muslim South Asia: Ed. Chris Shackle (1999); University of London Press.
The Arab Rediscovery of Europe: by Abu-Loghad Ibrahim (1963) Princeton University Press.
Living Islam: Akbar S. Ahmad (1993), BBC Books.
Discovering Islam: making sense of Muslim History and Society; Akbar S. Ahmed (1988), Rutledge, London.
Another Ireland: Maurice Ryan (1996), Greystone Press.
Turks, Moors and Englishmen: by Nabil Matar (1999) Columbia University Press.

Reference Notes /Bibliography

1.	Sharif, MM. A History of Muslim Philosophy (1963); 146-150, Wiesbaden: Otto Harrassowitz.
2.	Comerford, P. Islam and Muslims in Ireland: Moving from Encounter to Understanding; (2002) Search: Volume19: p89-93
3.	Phelan, A. Ireland by SEA (1998); 246, Dublin: Wolfhound Press.
4.	Muslims in Britain, a brief history (2005); p 2-3. Islamic Society of Britain and the Young Muslims UK publication, Birmingham.
5.	O'Connell, J. The Meaning of IRISH Place Names (1979); Belfast: Blackstaff Press
6.	Phelan, Andrew. Ireland by the SEA (1998); 32-41, Dublin: Wolfhound Press
7.	de Courcy Ireland, J. Ireland and the Irish in Maritime History (1986); Dublin: Glendall press.
8.	Goody, J. Past Encounters: in, Islam in Europe (2004); 42-44, Oxford: Blackwell publications.
9.	Matar, N. Soldiers, Pirates, Traders and Captives: Britons Among The Muslims; in Turks, Moors and Englishman: In the age of discovery (1999); 43-82, New York: Columbia university press.
10.	Visram, R. Asians in Britain; 400 years of History: London: Pluto Press.
11.	Fisher, Michael H. The Travels of Dean Mahomet, an Eighteenth Century journey through India; Edited with an introduction and biographical essay (1996): Berkley; University of California Press.
12.	Fisher, Michael H. Cork's Dean Mahomet: Journal of Cork Historical and Archeological Society, Vol. 101 (1996); 81-93.
13.	Kapoor, N. The Irish Raj (1966): Antrim; Greystone Press.
14.	Khan, Abu Talib. "MaAsir Talibi fi Bilad Afrangi". Volume 3; IOL British Museum.
15.	Khan, Abul Hasan Mirza. A Persian in the Court of King George, 1809-1810 (translated by MM Cloake, 1988); London; Barrie and Jenkins.
16.	Khan, Abu Talib. Travels of Mirza Abu Talib Khan in Asia, Africa, and Europe during 1799, 1800, 1801, 1802 and 1803 (translated by Charles Stewart 1814): London; Longman, Hurst, Rees and Orme.
17.	Said, Edward W. Culture and Imperialism (1993): New York; Alfred Knopf.
18.	Achmet, Dr. the Theory and Uses of Bath (1773); Dublin: J. Potts.
19.	Achmet, Dr. "To the Committee of Physicians and Surgeons ". Broadsheet of Proposed rules (1773): Dublin; Achmet.

20.   Ahmed, Akbar S. Living Islam (1993): London; BBC Books.
21.   Ahmed, Akbar S. Discovering Islam; Making sense of Muslim History and Society (1988): London; Rutledge.
22.   Ryan, Maurice. Another Ireland (1966):48-67. Belfast; Greystone Press.
23.   Goody, J. Islam in Europe (2004): 15. Oxford; Blackwell publications.
24.   Kapoor, Narinder. The Irish Raj (1966): p 15-19. Antrim; Greystone press.
25.   ibid. pp 65-66.
26.   ibid. pp 90-94.
27.   ibid. pp 151-152.
28.   ibid. pp 84-88.

Appendix I

Historical account of the establishment of The Islamic Society of Dublin (Islamic Foundation of Ireland

On 23rd January (Friday) 1959, a general meeting was held at Koinonia House with the purpose of deciding whether or not to form a Muslim committee, which would organize Friday Namaaz (Prayer), Eid Namaaz and some lectures. Thirty-three students of the Muslim faith and who belonged to various countries, gathered at the meeting. The matter was discussed and a vote was taken to finalize whether such a body was wanted or not. It was unanimously accepted to form the body. It was also agreed the functions of this body would be decided by the students (Muslims).
The following officials were elected:

Chairman: Mr. Hoosen Lockhat
Secretary: Mr. Yousuf Jhavary
Treasurer: Mr. Ismail Docrat
Committee of 8 members.
        Hoosen Lockhat
        Ismail Docrat
        Zakudeen Zaveri
        Ahmad Al-Atrash
        Yousuf Jhavary
        Ebrahim Mannah
        Harith Lamki (Later Consultant Gynaecologist at Royal Victoria Hospital, Belfast)
        Abdullah Al-Kathiri

Appendix II

Minutes of first COMMITTEE MEETING ON 7TH FEBRUARY, 1959

On Saturday the 7th February 1959 a committee meeting was held at Koinonia House, 33 Harcourt Street, Dublin. The committee sanctioned the holding of the Friday Namaaz (Prayer) and decided that Fasting time-tables should be printed for the forthcoming fasting season. The committee also decided that arrangements should be made for accommodating a large crowd for Eid Namaaz (Prayer). It was hoped that a name for the body would be decided upon at the next General meeting.

It was agreed at this meeting to print circulars and inform Muslim students, that prayers would be held on Fridays at Koinonia House and a circular announcing of a meeting to be held 17th April 1959 at Koinonia House, 33 Harcourt Street, Dublin (Circulars announcing meeting and also Eid Namaaz (prayer) – on 10th April were also distributed.)

One of the main purposes of holding this meeting was to ratify the name for the Muslim body, which was formed at an earlier meeting - on the 23rd of January 1959. At the meeting the following three names were suggested:-

1) Dublin Islamic Jamaat was suggested by Mr. Hoosein Jamal
2) Islamic Study Circle   "   "   "   Mr. Yousuf Jhavary
3) Dublin Islamic Society   "   "   "   Mr. Ragaa Makharita

Mr. Jamal withdrew his suggestion in favour of Mr. Makharita's suggestion. The majority voted for Dublin Islamic Society, and hence forth that name was adopted for the Muslim Body in Dublin.

It was decided at this meeting that there would be no subscription fee levied on anybody who participated in the activities of this society. If anyone did wish to donate any money to the Dublin Islamic Society, it would be accepted. It was emphasized that donations would be purely voluntary.

Later the Chairman, Mr. Hussein Lockhat, tendered his resignation due to ill health. Therefore, a new President was voted in, and a Vice-President was also elected since the new President intended leaving Dublin at the end of June, 1959.

The new President was Mr. Rajaa Makharita – proposed by Mr. Abdullah Al-Kathiri and was seconded by Mr. Ismail Docrat.

The elected Vice-president was Mr. Essop Ravat- Proposed by Rafiq Jhetam and was seconded by Mr. Yousuf Jhavary. (Mr. Ravat later became the President following the departure of Mr. Makharita from Dublin, in June 1960).

The Chairman, Mr. H Lockhat thanked everybody for their co-operation and brought the meeting to a close.
(From the Dublin Islamic Society's General Meetings Minutes Book 1974 and the web Page 'History of Muslims in Ireland').

The events to establish the Dublin Islamic Society in chronological order are as follows

1955-1959; a group decided to form an Islamic Society (Charity). They were: Mohammad Islam Khan, Fatima Chaudry Malon, Iftikhar Ahmad, Mohammad Saleh and Mohammed Mumtaz.

1960-1965; a group of ladies who were living in the Harrington Street area also formed an organization by themselves called the Islamic Centre. A gathering was held in No.7 Harrington Street and at 68 Lower Leeson Street Dublin.

Friday's prayers by that time had been taking place in rented flats or houses as well as mainly in Harrington Street where most of the accommodations were rented to students.

1965-1970; Numbers of students were increasing rapidly and the campaign to raise funds started in 1967/68. The requests were made to the authorities in Kuwait, Libya, Saudi Arabia, Algeria, UAE, Jordan and Islamic Centers in the UK for financial assistance in order to acquire a mosque in Dublin.

The establishment of an Islamic Centre in Dublin has been a long-cherished aim of the Dublin Islamic Society. In 1969, when Muslim students numbering over 100, along with several families of professional people and others who were permanently settled in Ireland (total of over 300), felt the need for acquiring a Centre incorporating a prayer hall with facilities for ablution and an Islamic library. A fund-raising campaign was initiated in 1969, directed mainly at parents and relatives of students studying here. The vigorous publicity that accompanied the fund raising campaign was initiated amongst others by Abdullah Lamki, Dr. Harith Lamki (who later became a renowned Gynaecologist in Belfast) and Dr. Abdul Rehman Ismail and maintained subsequently by others serving on the Islamic Centre Project Sub-Committee. .

In March 1971 the students formed an Islamic foundation called "DUBLIN ISLAMIC SOCIETY" (This is the date when the Society was registered as a Friendly Society.) and in October 1971 the following became the nominee of the Trustee for opening the accounts. They were the founding members of the society.

1)	Ebrahim Sayed,	(South Africa)
2)	Khalil Ravan	(?)
3)	Tazammul Hassan (Hussain) Hayat,	(South Africa)
4)	Mohamed Hanief Khan,	(India)
5)	Abdul Kader Bhabha,	(South Africa?)
6)	Abdol Haqq Suleman Kajee,	(South Africa)
7)	Fatima Chaudry Malon,	(Pakistan)
8)	Hamed Hussain Nasser,	(?)
9)	Hassan Kadwa,	(?)

Bank account was opened on trust in the Royal Bank of Ireland at the Grafton Street Branch.

Registered address was P.O. Box 548 Rathmines, Dublin 6 used for official purposes.

Dublin Islamic Society replaced the Islamic Centre (unregistered), but a number of Muslim ladies continued the activities as ladies charity.

Friday prayers continued to be held in rented accommodation in Rathmines or in a Club provided by the Garda. Although No.7 Harrington Street was purchased officially in 1974, but since 1969, prayers and gatherings were conducted from time to time in the upper part of the building.

In January 1972 a Mr. Salem Azzam on behalf of the Royal Embassy of Saudi Arabia from UK became involved in the society, and sufficient funds were raised to acquire a Mosque.

The envisaged amount required for the purchase of a modest property suitable for the purpose of an Islamic Centre was, thanks to Allah, realized.
Of the larger donations received were the following:

The government of Abu Dhabi	£1,518.00
His Majesty, King Faisal of Saudi Arabia	£17,914.28

In February 1973 there was a credit balance of about £18,300 in the Royal Bank of Ireland for the Dublin Islamic Society account available for the acquisition of a centre.

Mahmood Coovadia (Medical Student) was appointed as Trustee in place of Ebrahim Sayed.

Salem Azzam received confirmation from the Royal Embassy of Saudi Arabia to "go ahead" with the purchase as freehold of a property.

In April 1973 No.7 Harrington Street became officially the registered address of Society, but still on rental arrangement.

On 22 Nov 1973; the Society agreed to acquire the property from Gilbert Leon White and finally on 30 October 1974 the whole building including the basement, ground, first and second floors was purchased for the price of £10,870.

In November 1975 the following New Trustees were appointed:
(1) Tazammul Hussain Hayat
(2) Ahmed Goolam Mohamed Adam
(3) Dr. Ismail Coovadia
(4) Abdul Hamid Nasser
(5) Mahmood Y. Motala
In August 1976 The Society announced the official opening of No.7 Harrington Street as the Mosque of Dublin.

In December 1977 Mohamed Sadique Y. Omarjee was appointed as trustee.
In November 1978 Mr. Mazlam Mohd Zawawi was appointed as Secretary.

1977-1983; The space available at No.7 Harrington Street was not adequate to accommodate all Muslims praying during Friday prayers owing to the rapid increase in the number of students in Eire from abroad.

1981 the Ministry of Endowment and Islamic Affairs in Kuwait sponsored a full time Imam for the Mosque.

1983; A few years after the establishment of the first Islamic Centre and Mosque in Dublin, the Mosque became too small for the increasing numbers of worshippers. The Muslims in charge of the society started a second campaign to collect donations in order to establish a bigger Mosque. Individual donations and substantial assistance from Qatar and Kuwaiti Governments enabled the purchase in 1983 of the present building of the Dublin Mosque and Islamic Centre at 163, South Circular Road. The headquarters of the Society moved from Harrington Street to the newly acquired premises. The building at Harrington Street was later sold as it was no longer used as a mosque, and from the money it generated some Waqf (endowment) property was bought in the area of the new Mosque.

Sheikh Abdullah, Mosa Engelbrecht, Mohammad Marwan Sabbagh, Salem Azzam, Nabeel Hammad, Mamoun Mobayed, Ibrahim Adris (Idris Ibrahim) , Shaikh Yahya M. Al-Hussein, and Mudaffar Al-Tawash were appointed as trustees for acquisition of No. 163 South Circular Road.

In 1985; No.7 Harrington Street was sold to Argus Security Ltd.

In July 1990 the name of the Dublin Islamic Society was changed to the Islamic Foundation of Ireland.

1983-2005; Sheikh Yahya Al-Hussein being a very competent and well informed person, has led prayers at the Mosque since 1983 and has shown active commitment to the Muslims and Islamic community in the Irish Republic. He has been trying to keep the faith away from any political interference. His services to Irish Muslims in general and to the Dublin Mosque in particular are highly commendable.
(Taken and modified from Oxford Intelligent Library)

Appendix III

First Committee to consider establishment of an organization and a Mosque in Belfast

The office bearers appointed at the first meeting of the committee to form an organization in 1961 were as follows:

Mr. Ghulam Mohammad	President
Mr. Mohammad Yaseen	Secretary
Mr. Shah Dean	Treasure
Mr. Karam Hussain Khan	Member (Nephew of Lal Khan)
Mr. Ghulam Hussain	Member
Mr. Rehmat Ali Khan	Member
Mr. Fateh Mohammad	Member
Mr. Habib Ali	Member

The First Friday congregation was held in 1961 in a house on the Old Park Road and then in Wellesley Avenue. A gentleman by the name of Dr. Akhtar, who obtained his Ph.D from the Institute of Agriculture, Queens University, started this. He later returned to Pakistan to become Dean at the University of Agriculture, Pakistan.

The next serious attempt to form an association and establish an Islamic Centre was made in 1975 by post graduate students, university lecturers, doctors in training and businessmen. The following were made the office bearers and founder committee members of the standing committee to establish a Mosque/ Islamic Centre in Belfast.

Mr. Quamer Hossain	President
Dr. (late) Naseem Akhtar	Secretary
Dr. Yusuf Hanore	Treasurer
Dr. Omar. Faroukui	Member
Dr. Yunis Qureshi	Member
Mr. Mohammad Hanif (Late)	Member
Dr. Imtiaz Pathan	Member
Dr. Chaudhry	Member
Mr. Shah Dean	Member

Appendix IV.

First Trustees of Belfast Islamic Centre (1978)

Mr. Aslam Shams (chairman FOSIS)
Dr. Aslam Azzam (European Conference of Muslim Association)
Mr. Shah Dean
Dr. A.M.Siddiqui
Mr. Quamer Hossain (As President)

Trustees 1980-1982
Dr. Aslam Azzam
Mr. Quamer Hossain
Mr. Shah Dean
Dr. A.M. Sidiqui (As President)

Trustee 1982-1992
Dr. A. M. Siddiqui
Mr. Quamer Hossain (Resigned in 1992)
Mr. Shah Dean
President of the Belfast Islamic Centre (BIC)

Trustees 1992-1994
Dr. A. M. Siddiqui (Resigned in 1944)
Mr. Shah Dean
Dr. Mazhar M. Khan
President of Islamic Centre (Dr. Mamun Mobayad)

Trustees 1994-1997
 Mr. Shah Dean (Retired in 1997)
Dr. Mazhar M. Khan
Dr. M. Yusuf Hanore
President of the Belfast Islamic Centre (Dr. Mamun Mobayad)

Trustees 1997-2000
Dr. Mazhar M. Khan
Dr. M. Yusuf Hanore (resigned in 2001)
Dr. Zameer-ul- Huda
President of BIC (Dr. Mamun Mobayad)

Introduction to Profiles

The Research

This section was commissioned by the Al-Nisa Association Northern Ireland with the aim of producing a document which was both a celebration and acknowledgement of the substantial contribution made to Northern Irish society by members of the Muslim community. The research was also concerned with how and why people moved to and settled in Northern Ireland from elsewhere; the experience of living as a Muslim in Northern Ireland and how participants saw the future of the Muslim community in Northern Ireland. The material was compiled from both face-to-face interviews and self-completed questionnaires. (See Appendix 2). Those who participated are individuals and families of the Muslim faith who currently live, or previously have lived, in Northern Ireland.

The selection of participants is not and was not meant to be representative of the whole Muslim community in Northern Ireland. Those who took part, either volunteered or were nominated by someone else. However, the aim was to recruit a range of participants in terms of gender, age, country of origin and occupation. It was planned to interview approximately twenty women, twenty men and ten children or young people. In order to attract as wide a range of participants as possible, posters (See Appendix 3) requesting people to come forward were produced, along with letters (See Appendix1) and application forms. These were distributed widely amongst Muslim community organisations and individuals, including Al-Nisa, the Belfast Islamic Centre and the Northern Ireland Muslim Family Association. They were also circulated to the Education and Library Boards for display in local libraries, leisure centres, community centres, both of the universities in the Province and to hospitals.

The posters invited people to complete an initial questionnaire and contact details were given for further information. The closing date for inclusion was 27 May, 2005. It was agreed that Al-Nisa would select which applicants would be offered an individual entry in the book, with others being included in a directory. The response was initially slow, so a decision was made to extend the closing date. Also, the holiday period meant that people could be away for a number of weeks. Consequently, only thirty four face-to-face interviews were carried out and sixteen questionnaires were sent by e-mail. Nine of the e-mailed questionnaires were completed and returned. Of those who gave face-to-face interviews or completed questionnaires, there were five families where both parents and children were interviewed, five couples, thirty two individuals and five individual children or young people under the age of 25 years. Participants were given the opportunity to see the edited draft of their entry prior to printing.

Whilst the number of actual interviews and e-mailed questionnaires completed was less than the fifty aimed at initially, there were, in total, seventy one individuals who participated, ranging from 7 to 70+ years of age. Of these, there were twenty four adult women, thirty adult men, ten young women or girls and twelve young men or boys. The country of origin or background of participants represented thirty of Pakistani origin and nine of Indian origin. The other participants represented Bangladesh, Egypt, Iran, Iraq, Jordan, Lebanon, Mauritius, Palestine, Syria, Tunisia, Turkey and Sudan. Some areas were not represented, for instance, Afghanistan, the Philippines, Europe and much of the African continent. However, it was felt that, because the majority of Muslims in Northern Ireland would be of Pakistani origin, those interviewed reflected the overall picture.

In terms of occupational backgrounds, the largest group of participants were medical doctors (including: GPs, consultants, obstetricians, psychiatrists and surgeons); however, also represented were people from the worlds of accountancy, academia, the arts, business, education, journalism, law, media, teaching community and social work. Finally, many of the women interviewed had put their careers on hold in order to bring up their families.

Living in Northern Ireland

The context of the interviews is laid down in the previous section, which documents the long association of Muslims with the island of Ireland and, particularly, Northern Ireland. Without this backdrop, it could be supposed that people of the Islamic faith have only recently reached these shores. However, Dr Khan has clearly shown that Muslims have had an historical connection with this part of the world. Notwithstanding this, the settlement of Muslims in Northern Ireland has substantially been associated with the twentieth and twenty first centuries. Starting in the 1930s, the community has grown steadily and I had the privilege of interviewing people whose antecedents were amongst those early settlers.

For those people who were not born in Northern Ireland, coming here was often a decision based on practical needs such as study, training, employment or marriage. Only three interviewees stated that they actively chose to come to Northern Ireland because they wanted to. However, the reasons for deciding to settle here were based on the friendliness and helpfulness of people; close family ties; quality of life; quality of the educational system; the peacefulness; the weather and the beauty of the countryside. Comment was frequently made on the similarities between Northern Ireland and the various countries of origin of the people interviewed. The vast majority of those who took part were at pains to stress that they had found people from both sides of the Northern Irish community divide friendly and helpful.

Past

Understandably, some people were concerned about the conflict prior to moving here. However, of those who came during or before the 'Troubles', only a few felt that they had been directly affected and, even then, not that they had been directly targeted. Only one person mentioned having been in proximity to an explosion and another had his premises damaged when the shopping centre his business was located in was bombed. The feeling is that, because Muslims were seen as 'outside' the two main communities in Northern Ireland, they were left alone. Although, the common story of 'are you a Protestant or Catholic Muslim' has been mentioned by some of the interviewees. Of those working within medicine, many have treated patients who have been affected physically or psychologically by the 'Troubles' and at least three interviewees worked with victims of the Omagh bombing.

For some people, the existence of the army on the street added an element of familiarity, having come from somewhere where military presence is also part of everyday life, indeed one person commented that living in England seemed more abnormal for him for this reason.

Doctors who were here during the height of the 'Troubles' found that they were often let through paramilitary road blocks. Not understanding the nature of the divisions in Northern Ireland could on occasion, however, create difficulties. Nevertheless, there was a definite feeling that being seen as 'outside' could benefit both members of the Muslim and the local communities. There was a sense that the local community, in particular, welcomed the opportunity to communicate with someone without the complex process of finding out which side the other person was from.

Present and Future

The Peace Process and the road to peace has been both cause for celebration and concern. There is a feeling that once the two main communities in Northern Ireland stop fighting, certain elements of the wider community will look for someone else to 'pick on'. Related to this is the feeling that whilst the 'Troubles' were at their height, no one really noticed that there were people in Northern Ireland from other cultures. The coming of peace has meant the presence of minority ethnic communities here are now more evident, partially because more people are now moving here from other countries. There is a feeling expressed that the wider community not only needs to notice that there are people from different ethnic backgrounds here, but also to become more aware of different cultures and more accepting of difference.

Another concern is that, with the coming of peace, Northern Ireland may experience more of the problems which occur in other Western societies, such as drug use and high crime rates.

A major barrier to Muslims 'mixing' with the wider community is the focus on socialising in bars and the role alcohol plays in most social events. For some Muslims this is insurmountable but, for others, the presence of alcohol does not preclude attending an event. However, there is a need for greater awareness within the wider community of food which is acceptable.

The relatively small numbers of the Muslim community in Northern Ireland has, for some, been a positive experience, encouraging more interaction with the wider community and, therefore, a broader experience than members of some Muslim communities in England may enjoy. However, the small numbers of Muslims in some areas can mean isolation and lack of facilities. Dedicated premises for worship are lacking in areas outside Belfast and attempts to build them have met with hostility from some local communities. Whilst participants have been appreciative of organisations which make premises available for Friday prayers and other meetings and events, there is a real desire for somewhere which is specifically for the Muslim community; although most would say other people would be welcome to visit these premises.

Examples of institutional racism, stereotypes and assumptions have been mentioned. For instance, there is sometimes an assumption made that, if a person's ethnicity is not Northern Irish, they may not speak English. Some interviewees talked about more direct racism, such as name calling and criminal vandalism. Other participants mentioned that, whilst they had not experienced direct attacks, they knew of people who had.

Integration was seen as of central importance, however, it was stressed that this must be linked with maintaining one's own beliefs and culture. The question of who was held responsible for facilitating integration, however, varied. Whilst some saw integration as an equal responsibility between the Muslim and local community, others saw primary responsibility falling to one or the other. For most people, however, the need for both communities to move towards each other, learning from each other and accommodating each other was essential for a positive future. Particular areas which need to be addressed within Northern Ireland are, for example, the provision of female doctors for Muslim women patients, Religious Education in schools incorporating religions other than Christianity and access to GCSE's and 'A' levels in languages spoken within Muslim communities. None of the interviewees advocated separate educational provision for Muslim children. However, a need for supplementary provision was identified to ensure young Muslims are taught about their religion. Also seen as desirable was the provision of youth groups which addressed the needs of young Muslims.

A key concern mentioned was the need for unity within the community and, whilst many raised the issue of lack of facilities outside Belfast, there seemed to also be a desire for a centre which could be used by all Muslims in Northern Ireland.

The explosions in London, in July 2005, occurred about half way through the interviews and had a significant impact on the responses to the question about thoughts on the future. Without exception, there was condemnation and anger expressed about the bombs; however, there was also fear of the impact on perceptions of Muslims and how this could translate into a threat to Muslims living here. The media was held to have particular responsibility for the negative image of Muslims. In particular, how it portrays a stereotyped image of Muslims and seems to pick individuals who represent that stereotype, rather than the diversity that exists within the Muslim community both here and elsewhere. Striking parallels were drawn between this and the coverage of Northern Ireland where, for many years, the main images focussed on extremes and stereotypes also.

Prior to 7/7, people had also commented on difficulties brought about by changes in perception by the wider community since 9/11 and the portrayal of all Muslims as 'bad'. Some people commented that the use of the term 'Muslim' and/or 'Fundamentalist' was both inaccurate and unhelpful. Interviewees felt that, since Islam means peace, defining people as Muslim terrorists was contradictory. Similarly, the term 'Fundamentalist' should, it was said, be replaced by 'extremist'. Interviewees again made comparisons with Northern Ireland where the media would not use the term 'Protestant' or 'Catholic' terrorist.

Notwithstanding the above, participants were generally optimistic about a positive future for the Muslim community in Northern Ireland. Reference was made to the underlying friendliness and courtesy of the local community and hope was expressed that these characteristics will overcome the recent and worrying occurrences of attacks which have been reported.

I would like to thank all those who participated in this research. The people I interviewed were generous with their time and hospitality and those who completed the questionnaire showed consideration in the promptness with which they returned the completed version. I would also like to thank my mother and husband, who have taken on many additional responsibilities in the home to enable me to complete these profiles. I would further like to thank OFMDFM, Marc Steenson of Three Creative Company Ltd, my mother, Eileen sister and my husband, Andrew who have 'proof read' the document.

Finally, I would like to thank the members of Al-Nisa for their hospitality and providing the initial contacts. In particular, Mrs. N. Raza for the administrative support and feeding me, and Mrs. A. Khan for keeping me on track and her personal knowledge of the community.

Moira McCombe

Mr Ahsan Abbas

Mr Abbas lives in Holywood. He is married with four children: three boys and one girl who are twelve, ten, five and three years old. He is originally from Baghdad, Iraq and his wife is from Northern Ireland.

Living in Northern Ireland

Mr Abbas came here in 1978 to study Mechanical Engineering at the University of Ulster. He found people very friendly and, in particular, noticed that families are close here and play a big part in people's lives. This reminded him of Iraq.

For Mr Abbas, one of the main barriers to integration is a limited awareness of other beliefs and traditions. In particular, socialising can be difficult for Muslims because, in Northern Ireland, it often involves alcohol and bars and there is a perception that if you do not drink you are "a bore". He says:

"There are not enough cafes here or places where you just go to have a chat or have a good social life without having alcohol involved. I find this is a big obstacle between the Islamic community and the wider culture".

Another factor is that people can find it strange when Muslims take a few minutes during the work day to pray.

"If the time of prayer comes at work, people find it strange that you hide yourself away and spend three minutes to pray to God. If they understood our traditions and the way we practice our religion they would find this quite normal – in the same way, Christians may say 'I'm going to go into the church for five minutes or I'm going to light a candle'."

Achievements and Contributions

After finishing his degree, Mr Abbas started work in the building industry, designing heating, ventilation and air conditioning plants. Eleven years ago he started his own company in partnership with a Northern Irish man. His partner is on the electrical side and Mr Abbas is on the mechanical. Initially there were only the two of them, but now nine people are working for the company. They mainly deal with installing mechanical and electrical services in new buildings or renewing them for existing buildings.

A few years ago Mr Abbas decided to become more active in the Muslim community and, through the Northern Ireland Muslim Family Association, became involved in teaching children Arabic. He felt this was important,

55

especially for children from 'mixed marriages' who may only learn English. His children are bi-lingual and this was achieved through Mr Abbas speaking to them in Arabic and their mother speaking to them in English. This, he believes, is a big advantage because they are comfortable in both languages and will, therefore, find it much easier to integrate into Arabic society when they visit.

Thoughts on the future

Muslims, Mr Abbas believes, do want to integrate and, with an increase in appreciation and understanding of Islam, the gap between Muslims and the wider community will close. Mr Abbas hopes that, in the future, a greater awareness of and respect for different cultures and religions, would enable people to mix more and for Northern Ireland to become a truly integrated society.

Mr Khodr Abou Saleh

Mr Abou Saleh is originally from Beirut, Lebanon. However, he and his family moved to Cyprus during the war and he worked there for about eight years. He met his wife, who is from Northern Ireland, in Cyprus and they stayed there for four years before moving here. They have lived in Newcastle, Co Down, since 1986 in a house overlooking the sea.

Living in Northern Ireland

Mr Abou Saleh loves living here, saying: "I have lived here for longer than in Lebanon and it is my home". When he came here he was surprised by how friendly people were, especially because he was a 'foreigner'. An example he gives is of people saying good morning in the street. He feels he has been accepted by the community in which he lives; he has made many friends and has never experienced any problems here. Indeed, coming from Beirut, Mr Abou Saleh found Northern Ireland quite peaceful. In his work, he used to travel widely in Northern Ireland to areas associated with both communities and never had any problems, feeling he was, invariably, treated with kindness. Mr Abou Saleh enjoys hill walking and living in Newcastle is perfect for this. However, for the last three years, since starting his business, he has not had much time to walk in the Mourne Mountains, but still manages to walk on the beach regularly. He loves living in Newcastle and says that the community there is very mixed. He feels he respects people and they respect him.

Achievements and Contributions

When he first came here, Mr Abou Saleh worked as a Sales Representative for a publishing company. Eventually, he opened his own takeaway restaurant in Banbridge, where he employs local people and contributes to the local economy. In Lebanon, he worked for the family shipping business which was based in Beirut. He goes to Northern Ireland Muslim Family Association every Friday for prayers.

Thoughts on the future

Mr Abou Saleh's dream and hope for the future is that Muslims will become closer to the local community:

"at the end of the day we are all human beings and we all believe in God and the communities will become closer and the leaders will become more open. I have my religion and you have your religion but this shouldn't stop us getting on together."

Ms Uzema Ahmad

Uzema was born in Belfast and her parents were originally from Pakistan. By profession, she is a Chartered Accountant and is married to a Doctor. They have two children: Hassan, who is four and Nayha, who is one year old. The family left Northern Ireland in 2003 and now live on the Isle of Wight, where Uzema works as a part-time Auditor.

Living in Northern Ireland

Uzema says that she has never really had any problems living as a Muslim in Northern Ireland, but wonders if this may be partly because she does not wear hijab and, therefore, is not immediately recognisable as Muslim. However, she did experience people making assumptions about her on occasion. Her father had a shop in Lisburn and she remembers someone saying to her: "First time I've ever heard an Asian girl speaking with a Belfast accent". This was only a few years ago and it made Uzema wonder where that person had been living for the past twenty years. Similarly, when she first started work, some clients of the company would ask her manager: "Can she speak English?".

Achievements and Contributions

Uzema went to Belfast Royal Academy, achieving ten 'O' levels and four 'A' levels, before going to Queen's University. Whilst at school, she participated in the Duke of Edinburgh Award Scheme, achieving the Bronze, Silver and Gold Awards and attended the Gold award ceremony at Buckingham Palace. She was the first girl of Pakistani origin within the Muslim community here to attend Queen's. She graduated with a 2:2 in Maths and Computer Science Joint Honours in 1992. On finishing her degree she was offered a training contract as a Chartered Accountant with Coopers & Lybrand, which she completed. During her time with this company she audited the accounts for several large local businesses, such as the Hastings Group and W D Irwin & Sons, Ltd. She also audited the accounts of charitable and voluntary sector organisations, including NIPPA, the Church of Ireland Trust and the Royal British Legion. She worked with the company until 2002.

Until leaving Northern Ireland, Uzema was an active member of the Pakistani Muslim Community.

Thoughts on the future

For the future, Uzema would hope that Muslims be accepted and acknowledged by society. Although, in the context of Northern Ireland, she questions what hope is there for people from different ethnic backgrounds being accepted when "some Protestants cannot tolerate Catholics living in Northern Ireland".

She feels that September 11th and the recent London bombings have damaged the image of Muslims in both Northern Ireland and elsewhere.

Dr Niaz & Mrs Sarah Ahmed

Dr and Mrs Ahmed are originally from India. Dr Ahmed moved to Northern Ireland in 1973 to work, whilst Mrs Ahmed came here on her marriage. They live in Dungannon and have three adult children, two daughters and a son.

Living in Northern Ireland

It was someone's prejudice about the Irish that encouraged Dr Ahmed to come to Northern Ireland: he wanted to see what it was like here for himself. When he first came, the only person he knew was a GP in Newtownbutler. Dr

Ahmed has had many good experiences living here. He feels he has received respect and love from both communities and has never had any problems or experienced discrimination.

Achievements and Contributions

Dr Niaz Ahmed

In order to practice as a Medical Doctor in the UK, Dr Ahmed had to take a 'system assessment'. He took this in Manchester and it lasted a month. It was, he says, very difficult because he could not understand what people were saying due to the accent being completely different to those he was familiar with. Television was, he found, the best way to overcome this problem. Dr Ahmed passed the assessment and got a job in Doncaster in geriatric medicine but needed to do further training, so he completed a six month course in Internal Medicine in Edinburgh. He had just finished the course when he heard there was a vacancy at the Erne Hospital in Enniskillen so he rang the Consultant, Dr Sweeney, and:

"told him I had just finished the six month course and I had no money to come for the interview – would he interview me on the phone?"

Dr Sweeney, who was also the Vice President of the Royal College of Physicians in Dublin, decided to offer Dr Ahmed the post immediately. He worked in Enniskillen for a year and during that period, he and Dr Sweeney became good friends.

Dr Ahmed then worked at Craigavon and Mid-Ulster Hospitals, before moving to Dungannon in 1975 to work at the local hospital. Whilst there, he was offered some work by a local GP as a locum, covering from 9 am on Sundays until 3 am on Mondays. Through this, he found that he preferred working in General Practice:

"every case is a challenge – you are a 'Jack of all trades'. A GP is the first stop for patients; people rely on their GP, trust them and give them a lot of respect; a GP is their own boss".

Dr Ahmed is now semi-retired and working part-time. He says that working in General Practice can be tiring physically and emotionally and is not a "nine to five" job. He feels that it has changed since he first started and now quality of service is more important.

In his spare time, Dr Ahmed enjoys gardening, particularly growing herbs.

Mrs Sarah Ahmed

Mrs Ahmed has a BA (Hons) in Modern English Languages (English, Urdu and Hindi) and was a Teacher of English and Science before she moved to Northern Ireland. She says she was pushed to achieve academically by her grandmother, who had never been to school and, consequently, believed it was important for the girls of the family to have access to education. Mrs Ahmed was the first girl in the village to get a degree and she was also allowed to work. All her sisters are also highly educated and one of them has been elected as a member of the Council in Bihar, India.

While the children were growing up, Mrs Ahmed was a full-time mother. She says:

"I taught our children to believe in truth and respect others. Northern Ireland is their home. We are all human – we have to respect others".

The children are now all adults. The eldest, their son Waqar, graduated in Medicine from Queen's University and is now training to be a GP in Belfast. Waqar is also a Martial Arts champion. Aasia, who is the second eldest, graduated in Medicine from Aberdeen University and is now training as a GP in England. Sazie, the youngest, is in Glasgow studying to be a Pharmacist.

Since 1997, Mrs Ahmed has been active in the community and worked with several different groups. She was one of the founders of Dungannon District Women's Group, which was set up that year and a member of the Management Committee. She also worked as the Co-ordinator for a year. Since the group ended, she has started a new women's group for Craigavon, Banbridge and Dungannon. The new group runs classes in Urdu and Information Technology which are funded by the South Eastern Education & Library Board. The centre now has Urdu software and Mrs Ahmed hopes they will eventually have their own computer suite. She is also involved in the Women of the World group, teaches children Urdu on Sundays in Craigavon and works as a part-time Science Technician at the local Academy.

Thoughts on the future

Mrs Ahmed believes that the future relationship between the Muslim community and the wider community will continue to be good. She feels that Northern Ireland is a place where religious beliefs are important and that people here respect different religions.

Mr and Mrs Samir Al-Halabi

Mr Al-Halabi is originally from Lebanon and is married to "a girl from Northern Ireland". They met after he had finished his full-time studies and have three daughters aged thirteen, nine and eight. The family live in Belfast.

Living in Northern Ireland

Mr Al-Halabi came to Northern Ireland in the early 1980's to study. He had been studying English in London and wanted to do his 'A' levels, so his landlady, who was from Newcastle, Co Down, suggested he came here. He moved to Newcastle and lived there for two years. He liked it because it was quiet and there were no distractions. However, he did find the winter very cold and remembers seeing snow for the first time. When he moved there, he was one of the first "foreigners" and remembers people being very curious about him. Nevertheless, he found people were very friendly on both sides of the community.

As a Muslim, Mr Al-Halabi believes that Muslim children should not be isolated but should be given the opportunity to integrate and learn about other cultures. However, he also believes that it is important that they are aware of their identity as Muslims and their culture. He believes his children are too young to attend Religious Education classes in school because they could find it confusing.

Mr Al-Halabi has lived in Northern Ireland for over twenty-six years and has never experienced any problems, although some of his friends have. Generally, he feels the people of Northern Ireland "are the friendliest people you would ever meet – from both communities". Having come here when he was eighteen, Mr Al-Halabi has lived for most of his life in Northern Ireland and considers it his home.

Achievements and Contributions

After 'A' levels, Mr Al-Halabi studied for an HND and later a BSc in Civil Engineering at the University of Ulster. After his degree he worked for RJ Maxwell for almost three years and then moved to the Design Section of the Roads Service, where he still works. He is involved in designing both traffic calming and cycle route schemes.

Mr Al-Halabi is active in the Northern Ireland Muslim Family Association (NIMFA) and is a member of the Executive Committee. NIMFA works with other agencies to put forward the Muslim point of view, as well as providing support for Muslim families. He is particularly involved in the school, where children can learn Arabic, Islamic and Qur'anic Studies. One of the aims of NIMFA is to reach out to the wider community, so some of the summer activity programme events are open to all children.

Thoughts on the future

Mr Al-Halabi is hopeful of the Peace Process in Northern Ireland. He feels life is too short to keep fighting and it saddens him when he hears of people being killed. With time, he believes the differences will be resolved through talking and getting to know each other and hopes no more lives will be wasted.

He is concerned that, after the bombs in London, a minority of people may react against Muslims. He emphasises that what happened in London was completely wrong and that Islam is against killing, as are all religions. He believes that there is never any justification for killing. However, he also believes that we must try to understand "what made these kids do this thing" and the connection to what is happening internationally, such as in Iraq and Palestine. He is further concerned that what happened in London will put at risk one of the things that is valuable here – Freedom of Speech – which does not exist in all countries.

Mrs Al-Halabi

Mrs Al-Halabi has taken her husbands name in line with Northern Irish culture, although in Muslim societies married women generally keep their own surnames. This is, Mr Al-Halabi says, a sign of respect for women, acknowledging that they have and keep their own identity. Mrs Al-Halabi is from a 'mixed marriage' and says that her husband's religion was never an issue. She feels that their children do not have any problems being Muslim and some of their friends have attended NIMFA events. For Mrs Al-Halabi, there is a lot to admire about Muslim culture, including the emphasis on the family and the moral guidelines. Many of these, she feels, have been lost in Northern Irish culture, for example, respect for adults. She hopes, that in the future, "people can accept people from other cultures and beliefs whilst keeping their own".

Jasmine

Jasmine, who is thirteen, is good at Art and History and particularly enjoys Art. She is also learning Arabic, Spanish and Irish. Other than her academic subjects, Jasmine enjoys designing clothes, making jewellery and playing hockey and netball. Jasmine also likes animals, playing with her friends, trampolining and going to the cinema. At school, she helped to raise over £1,000 for the Tsunami Disaster. In the future she would like to be either a Fashion Designer or a Vet.

Nadine

Nadine is nine and is good at Maths, which is one of her favourite subjects and she also likes sport, particularly hockey. She was the only girl in a hockey team which won a competition and she received a medal for playing. She enjoys riding her bike with friends and is learning Arabic at NIMFA. Her class at school raised over £100 for the Tsunami Disaster.

Rowanne

Rowanne is eight years old. She is good at Maths and enjoys PE, especially basketball and trampolining. Outside school she likes playing with her friends and riding her bicycle. She likes animals and would like to be a Doctor, Teacher or Pop Star. Her class raised over £100 for the Tsunami Disaster.

Mrs Massaret Ali

Massaret is married to Liaquat and they have three children. Kaméil, who is fourteen years old, is the oldest and attends the Abbey Grammar School. He enjoys football and computers and is good at photography. Iffah, a girl of eleven, has just started Sacred Heart Grammar School and is very musical. She is on her third grade for the piano and is also learning the violin. Rafaél, the youngest, is a boy of eight. He attends St Ronan's Primary School and is learning the trombone. She and her husband moved to their current house at the end of 1986. It is an old railway house which they renovated in a village outside Newry. Massaret is originally from Pakistan but was brought up in Northern Ireland. Her husband, who is also from Pakistan, came here when they married.

Living in Northern Ireland

Massaret came to Belfast when she was just ready to start school. She lived there for a number of years and her father did 'door to door' business. She remembers him being one of the few people who had a car in their street. This was, she says, obviously needed - enabling her father to travel further and so benefiting the business. Her childhood in the Oldpark was, she says, "brilliant". The family moved to Wales for three years, where her father worked in a Coca-Cola factory. Her parents decided to come back, however, because they missed Belfast. Their next move was to Glengormley, where Massaret spent her teenage years and lived there until she married. Coming from "humble" beginnings, Massaret is proud that her family have done so well: one of her brothers is a Surgeon and one is a Businessman. She is also proud of her sister's children, who have all done extremely well.

She feels, because the Asian community here is so widely spread, things are better than in England because there is more contact with the wider community. Her children, she believes, have the "best of both worlds" through their involvement with both the Muslim and the wider communities. Massaret is very happy where they live now, saying:

"I can't speak for other Muslims because it probably depends on the area you live, but I have never had any problems, my neighbourhood is lovely. We live in a mixed area, there are both Protestants and Catholics, but we are the only Muslim family in our area. There are, however, other Muslim families in the nearby towns of Newry, Warrenpoint, Craigavon and Portadown".

Massaret feels she may as well have been born here, because this is all she knows. She has only been back to Pakistan twice and remembers the first time as being quite a culture shock.

"It was strange getting off the plane, I was thinking this is supposed to be my home land and yet at the same time I felt a stranger, but in a nice way – I am so used to Northern Ireland".

In contrast to people who have moved to Northern Ireland from warmer climes, Massaret and her children found the heat of Pakistan difficult to cope with.

Achievements and Contributions

After 'A' levels, Massaret was accepted onto the foundation year in Art and Design at the University of Ulster, Jordanstown. She went on to do a degree in Applied and Decorative Art and Design, specialising in fashion and textiles, at the University of Ulster, Belfast. After completing the Graduate Enterprise Programme, she started her own business in fashion design and textiles. She closed it when she had her children because it demanded too much of her time. When her youngest child started nursery, Massaret returned to work, this time teaching in the Art and Design Department at Newry Institute. Here, she teaches on the Foundation Diploma and the 'A' level Art and Design programmes. She also teaches recreational painting and drawing for the Workers Education Association.

Massaret keeps in contact with the Muslim community through visiting other families and, wherever possible, attending events and celebrations. She feels it is important, particularly for the children's sake, to keep in contact with their own community as well as their Irish friends. However, working all week and having three children to look after, means it can be difficult to be regularly involved, especially since the Mosque is in Belfast.

Thoughts on the future

She has some concerns about the pressures on children and young people now and the way it is seen as normal to go out drinking and taking drugs. She hopes that living in a country area might be that bit safer and healthier for her family.

Her main hope for the future is, however, that her family continues to be happy and content. "If our children are happy we are both happy", she says.

Mrs Gulnaz Amjad

Gulnaz was born in Northern Ireland and is married with three daughters who are nine, eight and five years old. Her eldest daughter is very good at English and her second eldest daughter is very good at Maths. She is not sure yet where her youngest daughter's talents lie, since she has just finished Primary 1, but says she is a 'chatterbox'. Gulnaz's husband is from Pakistan and the family live in Belfast, with her mother, in the house that she was born in. Her father passed away in 1983.

Living in Northern Ireland

Gulnaz's father, who came to Northern Ireland in 1931, was born in India, but later moved to Pakistan. He owned a clothing factory, but this closed when she was quite young. Her mother is also, originally, from Pakistan and moved here in 1969, after her marriage. She says: "it was a big change for my mum, because in those days there were very few people from other countries and it was quite difficult for her because she didn't speak much English".

It was only when Gulnaz started school that she learnt English, since she spoke her mother's language at home. Primary school was fine, but after starting secondary school she began to realise she was different. She felt some people did not really understand things like fasting, although her close friends did.

For Gulnaz, the experience of living as a Muslim in Northern Ireland has been fairly positive and she has found that people are generally very helpful and pleasant; however, she feels this is related to the area where someone lives. She has only experienced a few negative incidents over the years but since she has become more strict in her practice of Islam, for example, covering her head, she has had more comments made. She has also found that people assume that she can't speak English when they see her:

"they assume that I'm foreign – the dark skin and then the head covering".

Gulnaz suspects things may be more difficult now for Muslim children and teenagers because of negative media coverage and September 11th.

Achievements and Contributions

After her GCSE's, Gulnaz went to Wellington College to do her 'A' levels and then went to Belfast Institute to do an HND in Textiles. She has also completed an ECDL course and a management training course. Gulnaz and her husband own their own wholesale clothing business and she is responsible for doing the accounts.

She has been the Treasurer of Al-Nisa from the very start and is involved in their activities. In terms of the local community, she is involved in the Parent Teachers Association at her children's school and also takes part in functions to raise money for the school. She tries to use the opportunity of these events to introduce her own culture. At the annual Summer Fair, for example, Gulnaz does henna hand painting and has prepared Pakistani food for a Food Festival Night. Gulnaz and her husband benefit the wider community through their business which supplies local traders and retailers with stock.

Thoughts on the future

Gulnaz would like to see a place in Northern Ireland where all members of the Muslim community can go. Particularly, she would like somewhere for the young people where they won't feel left out, somewhere which focuses on Islam and Islamic culture. She feels that Al-Nisa is currently filling that gap:

"developing things for young people – helping them to gain the confidence and social skills to integrate – no matter what they do, where they go or who they meet, they will have the confidence to stand up and say what they want to say - to find their place in the world".

Al-Nisa is already organising sessions for young people which, she hopes, will encourage them to eventually be involved in the running of the organisation.

Dr Lulu Basheer

Originally from India, Dr Basheer is married with two children and lives in Belfast. Her daughter, who was born in India, has just finished her 'A' levels at Methodist College and plans to study Medicine in Edinburgh. Her son was born in Northern Ireland and is going to do his 11+ this year, hoping also to go to Methodist College.

Living in Northern Ireland

Dr Basheer moved to Northern Ireland about seventeen years ago, when her husband came to study for his PhD at Queen's University. She had not wanted to leave India and says it took her more than eight years to accept that she would be living here. Arriving in January, the main thing she remembers is how cold it was. Local information was an issue and for the first few years she did not eat meat because she did not know where to buy halal. Similarly, Dr Basheer's children attended a Catholic primary school because she had not realised that some of the Protestant schools also taught religion and she had wanted a school where her children would have spiritual and moral direction, which could then be supplemented at home.

It was ultimately Dr Basheer's studies which resulted in the family settling here. They were planning to return to India when her husband had completed his PhD, but she was offered funding also for a PhD and decided to stay to complete it. Dr Basheer has found people here very friendly and has never experienced any racist problems, although she wonders if this is because she does not cover her head and, therefore, is not identifiable as a Muslim. She feels it is not easy to bring up children as Muslims here because they are in a minority. However, she thinks it is easier now for young Muslims because there are more places to socialise which do not involve alcohol, such as cafes and the cinema. In contrast, it can be more difficult for older people because so much socialising happens in the pub. In India, socialising would be more family orientated and involve visiting people's homes. She feels people are so busy here, there is not always enough time to entertain at home because of the work involved.

Achievements and Contributions

Dr Basheer completed a BSc in Civil Engineering in India and then studied part-time for her MSc at Queen's University. When her daughter was four she started her PhD and completed this four years later. Civil engineering is not a subject which attracts many women in the UK but in India it is seen as a respectable profession. This is because it is very important for girls to be in a secure job where they will not be harassed. She says, however, the numbers of women studying it are increasing in both countries. Dr Basheer has worked part-time since her daughter was young and is now working as a post-doctoral Researcher. Her work is related to the durability of concrete and through her work she contributes to research publications within the Department. This research benefits the construction industry in Northern Ireland and so contributes to the economy here.

In terms of the Muslim community, Dr Basheer has only become involved relatively recently, having been a member of Al-Nisa's Executive Committee for the past five years. She would like to increase her participation in the future, when her family is more independent. Prior to joining Al-Nisa, Dr Basheer was active in the Indian community and volunteered for the Indian Community Centre. She has always taken part in voluntary work. Even as a student, she volunteered helping blind students and would be interested in doing something similar again. Dr Basheer is also involved in supporting her children's activities at school.

Thoughts on the future

Dr Basheer sees her situation here as similar to that in India, since Muslims are a minority in both places. She feels this should not be a problem because you can be British and be a Hindu, Jew or Muslim, but the recent occurrence of terrorism has made things more difficult and has created a fear of Muslims. She hopes that in the future people will get over this fear and be able to get on together, to live together and get on as normal human beings: to start thinking about similarities rather than differences. She feels that British society is fairly tolerant of different cultures and England is very mixed. Northern Ireland is not so mixed but she believes that the younger generation are more accepting of difference, perhaps due to travelling and interacting with other cultures. She also hopes that the local community will become more aware of Muslim beliefs and culture and take these into account, which will help a peaceful co-existence.

Mr Mustapha Benhassine

Mustapha is originally from Tunisia. He is married to Jane and they have two children, a son, Omar and a daughter, Sonia. The family live in Strabane.

Living in Northern Ireland

Mustapha moved to Northern Ireland on a permanent basis in 1980 after meeting and marrying his wife. He originally came here in 1978 to work as a French Language Assistant, teaching at a Belfast secondary school.

He says that he has had no difficulties being a Muslim in Northern Ireland believing that this is because he does not "advertise" his faith and maintains a low profile in relation to his beliefs. He strongly believes: "that my faith is a matter for me and my Creator and no one else". Mustapha says that, whilst he may not practice Islam as rigorously as others:

"I know in my heart that I am not harming anyone and neither am I likely to. Islam means peace and that is how I have conducted myself by being at peace with neighbours, colleagues and others".

Achievements and Contributions

By profession, Mustapha is a Deputy Children Services Manager in Strabane. He graduated with BA Degree in English and French from the University of Tunis in 1980. In 1995 he was awarded a Postgraduate Diploma in Social Work from the University of Ulster at Magee College, Derry and in 2000 completed a Diploma in Applied Social Learning Theory in Child Care from Queen's University, Belfast. Last year (2004) he finished his MSc in Applied Social Learning Theory in Child Care through research, again at Queen's University.

Mustapha has no involvement in the Muslim community in Northern Ireland because, as far as he is aware, there are no other Muslims living in Strabane. He is, however, involved in the wider Northern Irish community through his work at the family centre and in his capacity as Secretary of Strabane Ethnic Community Association. This association is a multi-ethnic group which supports people from minority ethnic backgrounds in the Strabane area and organises a range of activities, including educational courses.

Thoughts on the future

In terms of the future, Mustapha's hopes relate to the relationship between the wider community and both Muslims and other minority ethnic groups. He hopes that the wider community will come to understand that Islam does not represent a threat to anybody and also that:

"bridges can be built to ensure that people would look upon difference in more positive terms and to avoid 'scapegoating' certain sections of the community because of their different ethnicity or faith".

Dr Nizam Damani
MSc (London), MBBS(Pakistan), FRCPath (London), FRCPI (Dublin), CIC (USA)

Dr Damani, who is originally from Pakistan, lives in Portadown with his wife Laila, and two sons, Numair and Namiz, who are thirteen and nine years old, respectively. His wife is also a Doctor, working in Haematology. Both of the boys were born in Northern Ireland and are very musical. The eldest, Numair, has been composing music since he was ten years old. He has composed four pieces and one, 'Indian Monsoon', was played at Banbridge School Music Festival. He is learning the piano, guitar and violin. Academically they are both top of their class. Namiz goes to Bocombra School in Portadown and Numair goes to Banbridge Academy.

Living in Northern Ireland

Dr Damani came to Northern Ireland in 1986 to work in the Royal Victoria Hospital. He stayed in Biggert House, just off the Falls Road. Prior to this he had worked in London and Nairobi, Kenya. He had taken Part I of his MRCPath exam in Microbiology and needed experience as a Senior Registrar in order to do his Part II exam. He was reluctant to come to Northern Ireland, being aware of the situation here and planned to return to London once he had completed his training. As part of his clinical rotation, he worked in both the Royal Victoria and City Hospitals.

During the first year, he flew back to London weekly to complete the second part of his Masters in Clinical Microbiology. In 1989 he passed his exam, started work as a Consultant Microbiologist in Craigavon Area Hospital and got married, all within a three month period. Dr Damani found both communities very welcoming and warm and felt comfortable here. His wife also liked it here, so they decided to stay. With the birth of his children, the ties to Northern Ireland became even stronger.

Compared to London, Dr Damani believes the quality of life in Northern Ireland is better, the people are friendlier and he has a better standard of living. Since 9/11, however, he feels there have been more difficulties. Racial abuse was rare here, but now there is a perception, held by some, that all Muslims are bad. This has been perpetuated by the media and, in particular, the British media. He believes the media often projects negative images of Northern Ireland in a similar way. Immigration is also now an issue: previously immigrants were not seen as a threat, but this is changing. Still, he feels things are not too bad, at least in the circles in which he moves.

Achievements and Contributions

By profession, Dr Damani is a Clinical Microbiologist with a special interest in infection control. He joined Craigavon Area Hospital as a Consultant Microbiologist in 1989, covering the whole of the Southern Health and Social Services Board, developing the Infection Control Service and also microbiology services in several hospitals. He has been the Clinical Director of Pathology and Laboratory Services for the past eight years.

Locally, Dr Damani has sat on various committees in the Department of Health, Social Services and Public Safety, which impacts on the Health Services here. Of central importance is his membership of the Project Board set up by the Department of Health which looks at the strategic delivery of pathology services and makes recommendations for future delivery. He is also a member of the surveillance sub-group undertaking a strategic review of infection in hospitals. He has been the chairman of the Northern Ireland Microbiology Audit Group for the last four years and is an Honorary Lecturer at Queen's University, teaching both undergraduate and postgraduate medical students. Recently he has been elected onto the regional council of the Royal College of Pathologists, UK.

Nationally, Dr Damani is a member of the Clinical Services Committee of the Association for Medical Microbiologists in the UK representing Northern Ireland. He is the only member from Northern Ireland on the Working Party of the British Society of Antimicrobial Chemotherapy, which produces guidelines on the testing of antibiotics in the UK.

For three years he has been the Treasurer of the International Federation of Infection Control (IFIC), a non-religious, charitable organisation which aims to raise awareness about infection control globally, especially in developing countries. In his work with IFIC he focuses on countries where he knows the culture and sensitivities. He was the founder member of the Infection Control Society of Pakistan, visiting regularly to deliver training. Next year he will visit Pakistan to develop policies for the whole of country. Recently he has been appointed as the Editor of the newly launched International Journal of Infection Control.

Dr Damani has written several books. His book Manual of Infection Control Procedures has been translated into several languages. He has also made presentations at many national and international meetings as an invited speaker.

His contribution internationally has had a positive affect on the perception of others about Northern Ireland, counteracting misconceptions. When he goes to conferences he talks about Northern Ireland and challenges the myths other people have of here. In this sense, he could almost be seen as an unofficial ambassador for Northern Ireland.

Thoughts on the future

For Dr Damani, it is crucial that bridges are built between Muslims and the wider community, particularly for the second generation to have a positive future. Integration is the key and he feels, realistically, this will fall to the Muslim community to reach out since they are in the minority. Integration starts at school and he feels that lessons should be learnt from Northern Ireland about the damage that a segregated education system can do in maintaining divisions.

"To have a positive future in Northern Ireland we need to integrate. We need to keep our culture, just like the Irish in different countries but we must also integrate. I am not saying we should adopt all Irish culture but we should try to take on the good from all cultures. It is a beautiful country and people and I believe we need to break the barriers while maintaining our culture."

Dr Omar & Mrs Khadija Farouki

Dr Farouki

Dr Farouki spent his early childhood in Palestine, but his family had to leave there when he was still quite young. They then moved to Egypt, where he continued his schooling. His wife, Khadija is from Syria and they have been married since 1990. They have two children, Rudaina, a girl who is twelve and Ridwan, a boy, who is ten and live just off the Antrim Road, in Newtownabbey.

Living in Northern Ireland

Dr Farouki came to Northern Ireland in 1967 when he was offered a post here. He says: "it seemed a good place so I came here". This was before the 'Troubles' had started and he says that he found the people here "friendly enough". However, he found it quite disturbing after the 'Troubles' had started and particularly during the 1970's and 1980's.

When Dr Farouki first came here there was no Islamic Centre, so people met for prayers in each other's homes and the numbers of those meeting were in single figures. Around 1969/1970 Queen's University Students' Union provided a room for prayer. However, the room was not very suitable because of the smell of beer from the night before.

Achievements and Contributions

The first degree Dr Farouki completed was at Oxford; he then went to the USA to complete his PhD and also taught there for two years. When he came back to the UK he started looking for work and was offered a post in Queen's University as a Lecturer in Civil Engineering and was later promoted to Senior Lecturer. He remained at Queen's throughout his working life, retiring in 2002. He is currently listed in Who's Who in Northern Ireland.

Dr Farouki was instrumental in establishing, what is now, the Belfast Islamic Centre and was President between 1985 and 1986. The Muslim community firstly raised enough funds to buy a house in Eglantine Avenue, which they then sold in order to purchase the current premises in Wellington Park. Dr Farouki is now involved in the Northern Ireland Muslim Family Association (NIMFA), participating in the workshops and other activities which they organise. He says that there are now between forty and fifty Muslims who come for Friday prayer but for Eid they have to hire a hall. They also organise meals to break the fast during Ramadan. Dr Farouki enjoys reading and walking in his spare time and used to play squash when he worked at Queen's, being a member of one of the league teams and playing competitively.

Thoughts on the future

Dr Farouki hopes, in the future, that there will be a better understanding of Muslims and Islam among the people of Northern Ireland. He is enthusiastic about members of the Muslim community giving talks about Islam and Arabic culture in schools and other places, feeling that this would help people to start to appreciate different cultures from around the world. He emphasises that he does not just mean talks about Arab culture but also others, such as Pakistani culture. Dr Farouki believes that this type of interaction will help people to know about Islam and Muslim countries and, through greater understanding and appreciation, will challenge some of the prejudices which exist.

He believes that Islam has a lot to offer the wider community. The values it promotes, for example, concerning morality, justice, respect and family relationships, could benefit Northern Irish society. There is a sense, he says, that:

"society here is losing its moral values and social cohesion – Islam can influence positively in morality and social aspects, such as respect for teachers".

He goes on to say that because Islam is based on reason, it needs to be believed through reason, not just accepted on blind faith. This is supported by the knowledge contained in the Qur'an, which has only recently been recognised scientifically. To highlight this, Dr Farouki gives the example of verse in the Qur'an about the formation of the human embryo.

Mrs Farouki

Living in Northern Ireland

Mrs Farouki came to Northern Ireland during the Gulf war, when she married Dr Farouki. She sees Northern Ireland as the family's home and admires the involvement of everyone in civil society. She feels that Northern Ireland is very rich in organisations which address a wide range of needs. She also feels that having a positive character and attitude makes things easier.

Achievements and Contributions

In Syria, Mrs Farouki had trained as an Architect and worked in this profession for ten years before she married. Although now a full-time wife and mother, Mrs Farouki is also involved in Al-Nisa, NIMFA and MCRC. She has also taken English and computer classes. In her role as a mother, she has aimed to bring up her children to show, by good example, what it is to be a Muslim.

Thoughts on the future

Mrs Farouki believes that the media should change the way it portrays Muslims, which is usually very negative. She feels real religion is absent here and there are a lot of difficulties in Northern Ireland with young people. She worries about these influences on the children.

Rudaina

Rudaina attends Victoria College and, before this, was a pupil of Cavehill Primary School. She was a champion Chess Player in the under twelve age group in Northern Ireland. The school she attends encourages the pupils to take responsibility for the environment. Rudaina is a Green Officer, which is a counsellor for the environment, and involves making sure the school is tidy and pleasant. Part of her responsibility is for recycling. She can both read and write Arabic and has some knowledge of French. Rudaina enjoys playing netball, using the computer and internet and is learning the piano. She is very artistic and is top of her class in Art at school. In the future, she would like to be a Psychologist or an Environmentalist.

Ridwan

Ridwan recently left Cavehill Primary School and is now at Belfast Royal Academy. He is very good at Maths and sat his 11+ at ten years of age. He is also a champion Chess Player in the under ten group in Northern Ireland and plays football. He enjoys computer games and his teachers sometimes ask him questions about computers. He thinks he may like to be a Scientist or Mathematician when he is older.

Dr Mohamed Fawzy & Mrs Afaf Aly

Dr Fawzy and his wife, Mrs Afaf Aly, are originally from Egypt. By profession he is a Consultant Radiologist and Mrs Aly is a Television Director. There are four children in the family, three boys and a girl. The oldest is Moutaz, who is seventeen; Karim is next and is fifteen; Ahmed, is seven and their daughter, Aya is aged eleven years old. The family live in Lisburn.

Living in Northern Ireland

Prior to moving to Northern Ireland to work in 1996, Dr Fawzy had been in London since 1993. He was initially offered a one year contract at Altnagelvin Hospital, which was then extended and he ended up staying in Northern Ireland. After Altnagelvin, he moved to Belfast to work in the training hospitals, that is, the Royal Victoria and Belfast City Hospitals, where he stayed for five years. In 2003, he was offered a permanent job in Craigavon and the family have lived in Lisburn for six years. He feels people settle here almost by accident, coming for a specific reason, then deciding to stay.

"you come by accident, but you don't decide to stay by accident".

Having previously lived in big cities, Londonderry was a new experience and different style of life for Dr Fawzy. He has found very little racism in Northern Ireland, although he thinks that in larger places, such as Belfast, there may be more. He has found that relations in the area where they live are very good, particularly with their neighbours.

Achievements and Contributions

Dr Fawzy started his training in Egypt, passing his basic Medical Degree in 1980, followed by an MSc in Radiology in 1987. He became a Fellow of the Royal College of Surgeons in Dublin in 1998 and a Fellow of the Royal College of Radiologists in London in 1999. As a Registrar, he entered the Porters Prize competition in 2002. This competition is for research undertaken by Registrars in Northern Ireland and his research into nuclear medicine earned him first prize. In his current post, as Consultant Radiologist at Craigavon Area Hospital, he focuses on nuclear medicine, which is his sub-speciality within radiology.

The main contribution Dr Fawzy believes he makes to Northern Irish society is through his job as a Doctor of Medicine with both his patients and colleagues. He is a member of the Northern Ireland Muslim Family Association, contributing to their activities and attending workshops.

Thoughts on the future

For Dr Fawzy, his hopes for the future are that the Muslim community will integrate into Northern Irish society and also that they will be accommodated. He feels the main problem is the media, which portrays a negative view of Muslims, focussing on extremists. He points out that every country or religion has extremists, but showing this as the 'norm' gives a bad impression.

He also hopes, in the future, there will be a centre for the whole of the

Muslim community. In such a place, the community could hold ceremonies and marriages, celebrate big events in Islam, hold meetings and have classes in Islam for children, which would complement their school education. Dr Fawzy says, at present, there are various small places, but not a central place, "even the Mosque is just a house and this is not suitable". He cites the growing Muslim population, which he estimates as being between four and five thousand, in support of this view. He believes that the community needs a clear vision and to work together to achieve this aim. They will also need to lobby politicians for support and, perhaps, apply for sponsorship from some of the wealthy Gulf States. For Dr Fawzy, such a centre would bring all the community together in one place rather than being split into many small communities.

Mrs Afaf Aly

Living in Northern Ireland

Mrs Aly came to here to join her husband when her daughter was three months old and her youngest son, Ahmed, was born in Derry. She is happy in Northern Ireland, finding people very friendly and believing that the Muslim community is safe here. She particularly likes the area they live in. At first she felt homesick but the friendliness of people here reminded her of people in Egypt. The children also like Northern Ireland and are happy in school.

Whilst some people show great consideration, for instance, a local school offered a room for prayer; she does feel that others do not know much about Muslims. Particularly after 9/11, she feels, Muslims were portrayed as killers or bad people and now, she says: "people are afraid of Muslim people". Mrs Aly is critical of the media for choosing to portray stereotypes instead of ordinary, average Muslims.

She feels that it is important to give the correct information about Islam starting at school, for instance; about Ramadan, why girls start wearing scarves or that Muslims believe in Jesus and the Prophets. People sometimes ask Mrs Aly why she wears a scarf and she points out that the Virgin Mary wore a scarf and so does Queen Elizabeth. She finds it hard to understand people having prejudices against those from different religions because in Egypt, Muslims and Christians live very well together and celebrate each others festivals. She says its not that they have any problems here, but she would like people to know more about Islam and Muslims.

Achievements and Contributions

Before coming here, Mrs Aly worked for ten years as a Television Director for Channel Five in Alexandria, Egypt, producing programmes on politics, women's issues and children. She worked with the Prime Minister and Secretary of State for Agriculture and for UNICEF, making programmes on women's health and family planning. She also worked on a project with Munich University, making a programme about children. Mrs Aly currently works as a Journalist for an international news journal in Egypt, the Egyptian Weekly Journal. She reports on politics and culture in Britain and Ireland and the Muslim community in Northern Ireland, as well as the inter-relationship between people from other countries and the local community. More recently, Mrs Aly has been involved in a project with Wallace High School (where the two oldest children attend) about the Lord Mayor of Belfast.

Mrs Aly raises awareness about Northern Ireland in Egypt through her journalism and tries to raise awareness about Muslims here through giving talks in schools.

Now the children are older, Mrs Aly is planning to return to Directing. She says she is missing her work and it is a shame to waste the experience and skills she has. She hopes to make programmes for children and documentaries.

Thoughts on the future

Mrs Aly wishes for peace in the future for Northern Ireland and for the media to start portraying a more representative and fairer image of Muslims.

Moutaz

Moutaz attends Wallace High School and will be doing his 'A' levels next year. He plays hockey for South Antrim Hockey Club and is learning to play the drums. He would like to be a Pilot.

Karim

Karim also attends Wallace High School and plays for the school hockey team. Outside school, he plays for Derriaghy Football Club and South Antrim Hockey Club. He will be doing his GCSE's next year and would like to be a Doctor.

Aya

Aya passed her 11+ and will be starting Wallace High in September. She does gymnastics at the Grove Centre and is in the hockey team at Friends Preparatory School. She would like to be an Architect and her favourite colour is pink.

Ahmed

Ahmed, was born in Derry and now attends Friends Preparatory School. He plays football at Laurel Hill Sports Club and also plays hockey. He thinks he would like to join the Police.

Mrs Yasmeen Hanif

Mrs Hanif's parents were originally from Pakistan, although she was born in Belfast. By profession she is a Nursery Nurse, and currently works part-time in a call centre while bringing up her family. Yasmeen has been married to Majid for five years and they live in Belfast with their two sons, Zain who is four and Adil who is two.

Living in Northern Ireland

Yasmeen describes herself as having been a "typical Irish girl" and finds it hard to describe growing up as a Muslim in Northern Ireland, because that is all she has known. She feels her parents were fairly 'relaxed' and she was allowed quite a lot of freedom. When she was growing up she lived with her parents, grandparents, aunt, uncle, three cousins, two brothers and one sister in a three bedroom terraced house in Belfast. It was only when she was a teenager, that the family moved to a large house in Cultra and Yasmeen can remember thinking "I'm in Dallas now". The whole family was involved in the retail business and Yasmeen used to have to spend her holidays and weekends working in their clothes shop. She remembers her grandfather bought a Rolls Royce. However, he eventually had to sell it because no one would go out with him in it because they were too embarrassed.

Her parents eventually moved into their own house and Yasmeen describes this as feeling 'weird', having been so used to being surrounded by people. Even now, with her own home and family, she finds she sometimes misses the 'hustle and bustle', and is often over in her mother's house.

About seven or eight years ago, Yasmeen started to wear hijab and felt that when she had her head covered she was given more respect; for instance, in bus queues, people would stand back to let her go first. However, she also found that people assumed she could not speak English. She has stopped wearing it at present, but hopes to start again in the future as she feels it is also a symbol of belonging. She believes that people in Northern Ireland are now more interested in Islam and will ask questions about it.

Achievements and Contributions

Yasmeen had some difficulties at school because, when she started, she was not fluent in English. This was because it was not the language spoken at home. As a consequence she was kept back in Primary I for two years and had to sit her 11+ when she was in Primary 6. It was not surprising, in these circumstances, that she did not pass the selection exam. Yasmeen attended Bangor Girls High School and then went to Holywood College to train as a Nursery Nurse. After working in several day care nurseries she went to America when she was twenty-three to work as a Nanny and to study childminding. She remembers her mother telling her before she left: "I know people fall in love, but if you do, make sure it's a Muslim". However, she only stayed in America for three months because she was so homesick for her family.

She sees her two main achievements as her children and discovering Islam. Although brought up in the Muslim faith, it was not until the death of Princess Diana that Yasmeen started to reassess her life and began to learn more about

Islam. She started attending the Mosque at Belfast Islamic Centre (BIC), but was worried she would be judged because she did not know very much about Islam. Although she was taught to read the Qur'an in Arabic, she could not understand it and she was not encouraged to ask questions. She met three women at the Mosque, Mrs Khan, Mrs Raza and Mrs Sabir, who took Yasmeen under their wings and started to teach her about Islam. She says that until this time, she had not realised the beauty and freedom of her faith. Through attending BIC, Yasmeen got involved in Al-Nisa and started to attend their classes. Yasmeen has been involved in Al-Nisa since it started and, except for a few years when she had her children, has held the post of Secretary. She still attends classes in Islam and is now learning Arabic. She also speaks a little Punjabi and Urdu.

Yasmeen feels that if she had stayed in America, she may never have discovered Islam because, to avoid isolation, she would have had to force herself to fit in with her friends, even though she would have felt uncomfortable. She says she: "I feared segregation from my friends if I didn't fit into their lifestyle".

Thoughts on the future

For the future, Yasmeen hopes that both Mrs Khan and Mrs Raza will get the recognition they deserve for all their hard work and contribution to the Muslim community. She would also like there to be a proper Mosque and school where adults and children can learn about Islam and Muslim culture.

As for her two boys, Yasmeen wants them to grow up to be good people and good Muslims. She believes the most important thing is that they should love God because this will ensure they have good character and everything else follows on from this.

She feels people are now less afraid of God or judgement and this has had a negative impact on society. She ultimately hopes that the world will one day live in peace, saying: "why fight over possessions when you can't take them with you?".

Dr Mohammed Yousuf Hannore

Dr Hannore is originally from India. He is married with three adult children, two daughters and a son. By profession he is a Mechanical Engineer and he and his wife live in Belfast.

Living in Northern Ireland

The reason Dr Hannore came to the UK was to continue his studies. He was offered a Teaching Assistant post in the Mechanical Engineering Department of Queen's University, Belfast, which he accepted and moved here in 1971. He completed both his MSc and PhD Degrees and was offered a post in a company specialising in aerospace and defence, based in Belfast and remained with them for over twenty-three years.

The family were happy here and the children, especially, were reluctant to return to India, particularly because the weather did not suit them there. Dr Hannore found people in Northern Ireland very friendly and accommodating, so decided to settle here permanently.

He has never personally experienced any difficulties with the local community here, either at work or in public, having found people in Northern Ireland to be both very considerate and helpful.

Achievements and Contributions

Dr Hannore was one of the founder members of the Belfast Islamic Centre (BIC), which was set up with the aim of catering for the religious needs of Muslims resident in the whole of Northern Ireland. He says that it was a slow process, particularly in the beginning, with some members of the Muslim community and, in particular, parts of the business community, expressing reservations. However, at a meeting called in the summer of 1974, it was decided to set up a Standing Committee for the establishment of an Islamic Centre in Belfast. The objective of the Standing Committee was to draft a constitution and to raise funds by approaching Muslims living in Northern Ireland, the rest of the UK and abroad. Dr Hannore became Treasurer and later Secretary of the Executive Committee of BIC, which was formed in 1976. He continued to be an office bearer of the Executive Committee until 1986/87, when the present premises of the centre were bought and refurbished. At the 1995/96 Annual General Meeting, Dr Hannore was elected to the position of permanent Trustee of the Centre, from which he resigned in 2002.

In terms of contribution to the wider community in Northern Ireland, Dr Hannore's main contribution, he feels, was through his teaching and academic research at Queen's University and his employment in the aerospace and defence industry.

Thoughts on the future

Despite the recent bombings in London having created certain misgivings about Muslims amongst the local community, Dr Hannore hopes, that given time people here will:

"realise that Muslims in general are peace loving people and that it is only a tiny minority who are responsible for these senseless bombings".

He points out that all Muslim leaders and members of the Muslim community have: "not only distanced themselves, but also expressed outright condemnation of this deplorable act".

From his experience, gained over the last thirty-four years living in Northern Ireland, Dr Hannore is confident that, in time, things will get back to normal.

Dr Irfanul and Mrs Ishrat Hassan

Dr and Mrs Hassan are from Pakistan and now live in Omagh. They have four children, two daughters: Huma and Sabah and two sons: Nauman and Abdul Rahman.

Living in Northern Ireland

Dr Hassan came to England to undertake further medical training. Whilst waiting to sit a competency test in English and Clinical Medicine, he visited his brother-in-law, who was working at South Tyrone Hospital in Dungannon. He found that he liked the environment and people were very friendly, so after passing the test, he returned to Dungannon and was offered a job at the same hospital.

Recently, Dr Hassan feels there have been changes in local attitudes related to the increased migration to the area for work in factories. This has altered the perception of local people who believe their jobs are being taken, even though vacancies have been difficult to fill locally. This has not, so far, been the case with doctors, possibly because people can see that they are needed. He believes that the situation is being exploited by ill-meaning people, causing tensions in the area and aggressive acts against immigrants, which he finds disturbing. However, Dr Hassan stresses that the majority of people here are friendly and it is only a small minority who are committing these crimes. Personally, he has experienced nothing but help and co-operation from the local community.

Dr Hassan believes that since the bombings in London "a cloud hangs over all Muslims". He stresses that Islam forbids the taking of life and, specifically, an innocent life:

"it is most heinous of people, it doesn't matter what their motives are, to take a life, especially of innocent people going about their business. The people who did this are using Islam as a shield and the Western media are stirring up hysteria against Muslims with the result that there has been a backlash."

The backlash, he feels, is not so prevalent in Northern Ireland as England, where Mosques have been attacked and Muslim women spat at. Dr Hassan has concerns that the negative feelings against Muslims may affect the future of his children and feels the whole community is being targeted for what are criminal acts of a few and which do not represent Islam.

Achievements and Contributions

Dr Hassan worked as a duty Hospital Doctor in Dungannon for almost six months before gaining a place on a three year Vocational Training Scheme for General Practice. During this training, he worked at Daisy Hill Hospital, Newry and at a GP's surgery in Warrenpoint. After completing his training he passed his postgraduate examination in General Practice, MRCGP and also his DRCOG in the same year. While working as a locum in Newry, he was offered a partnership in a surgery in Omagh. After three years he was offered a full partnership, becoming a principal partner in 1981.

In addition to working as a GP, Dr Hassan has continued to study and is involved in a range of other activities. He tutors fourth and fifth year medical students and is involved in training young doctors in General Practice, sitting on the Post Graduate Committee of the Northern Ireland Medical Council as the GP representative. He also advises the Department of Health on the needs of patients from minority ethnic backgrounds and is a member of the BMA Committee for Ethnic Minorities which advocates on the needs of ethnic minority patients.

Dr Hassan sits on a range of committees, locally and nationally, involving both medical practice and politics. He is an Audit Facilitator for the Western Health and Social Services Board and the Western Division Representative on the Northern Ireland Audit Committee, as well as Honorary Secretary of the British Medical Association's Western Division. Additionally, Dr Hassan is an active member of the local Medical Committee, which ensures the Government and Board adhere to such regulations and contracts which are in place. Finally, he represents the interests of GP's in the West of the Province through his membership of the Western Division of the General Practitioners Committee of the BMA and was Honorary Secretary of the Overseas Doctors Association.

He was actively involved in treating victims of the Omagh bombing and setting up counselling services for those affected. This led to the development of the Institute of Counselling in Omagh which gives training recognised by Queen's University. The expertise developed in Omagh has been used both in New York and Spain.

Other initiatives include the establishment of a community led Cardiac Service which enables patients who have been discharged from hospitals to get help within the community, including a monthly support group held in the local leisure centre. This was one of the first of such projects in either Northern Ireland or Britain. More recently he has started a residential project for alcoholics, staffed by ex-alcoholics and using a medical model. This is the first project of its kind in Northern Ireland.

The level of respect Dr Hassan is held in was demonstrated when he was voted 'GP of the Year' in 2002 for both Northern Ireland and the UK. This award was in recognition of the innovations he has put in place as part of his work.

Dr Hassan is the Auditor for the Northern Ireland Muslim Family Association (NIMFA) and tries to attend major events; however, because it is so far away, it is difficult for him to attend regularly. He is involved in supporting the local community of Muslims, especially 'overseas doctors', many of whom now come from the extended European Union and Arabic countries. He also speaks in schools about Islamic beliefs and values to raise awareness amongst the local community.

Thoughts on the future

In terms of the future, Dr Hassan has some fears about the increase of racism and concerns about the negative image of Muslims which is being promoted. His hope would be that these things will eventually disappear and the local community will become more aware about what Islam really means.

Mrs Ishrat Hassan

Mrs Hassan came to Northern Ireland in 1978 to join her husband. The journey was not easy, because she was travelling with her two eldest children, both of whom have learning disabilities. Initially she was quite lonely and managing the children was hard without family support. Although she had learnt English in Pakistan, some words were different here and communication could sometimes be difficult.

Since coming here, she has been involved in voluntary work, including Riding for the Disabled and Mencap. She is also a Trustee of NIMFA and a member of the Omagh Ethnic Community Support Group which organises activities within the area; including an annual Culture Show and a Multi-Cultural Fashion Show.

Nauman

Nauman is the eldest son and also the eldest child. He lives at the Positive Future Community in Lisnaskee during the week, but comes home most weekends. He goes to College where he learns cooking and studies computing.

Huma

Huma is the eldest daughter and currently attends the Omagh Centre. Here she takes part in activities such as cooking and is learning computing. She enjoys music and ironing, the latter of which is a great help to the family.

Sabah

Sabah is the younger daughter. She qualified this year as an Optician and is currently doing locum work. She is very musical, having achieved fifth grade on piano and third grade on the flute.

Abdul Rahman

Abdul Rahman is the youngest son and has just finished his 'A' levels. He will be leaving Northern Ireland shortly to take up a place at the University of Central Lancashire to study Physiotherapy. He is very health conscious and enjoys cycling and running.

Dr Mudawi A and Mrs Nejwa Hassan

Dr Hassan is as an Obstetrician who is originally from Sudan. He initially came to work in the Republic of Ireland; moving to England, where he stayed for eight or nine months, before coming to Northern Ireland in August 1999. He is married to Nejwa, who is also from Sudan and they have four sons aged fifteen, thirteen, twelve and seven years old. The three younger sons are interviewed below.

Living in Northern Ireland

Dr Hassan came to Northern Ireland originally to complete his postgraduate studies and "to have more exposure and experience" in terms of his profession. Although he would have few problems finding work in his field elsewhere, he prefers to stay in Northern Ireland. He decided to stay because he and his wife found it a pleasant place to live. He finds people here friendly and likes his work; also his children have settled well in their schools and have made friends. For these reasons, he cannot see any reason to move. The family try to go back to Sudan regularly to maintain the connection there and the children are learning Arabic.

There was a need for some adjustment on moving to Northern Ireland, particularly getting used to the weather. The food is also a bit different but they can find many things here.

"Northern Ireland is quite different from Sudan. Sudan is hot, Northern Ireland isn't; it rains and is very cold during the winter time. The type of food is a bit different but now-a-days everything is available, for instance, there are some Eastern and Mediterranean shops here and things we can't get here we can find in London".

Achievements and Contributions

Dr Hassan's original training was in Sudan and he worked for a period in Saudi Arabia, the Republic of Ireland and England. He has completed his postgraduate studies and finished the requirements for membership in his sub-speciality, Maternal Health. This involves health education for pregnant women, including that of unborn or new born babies. He says that, while he was completing his studies, he received great support from where he worked. Dr Hassan feels his work is a particularly positive branch of medicine, because there is usually a positive outcome, however, he finds it very sad when things do not work out.

He first worked in the Route Hospital, Ballymoney, which is now closed and stayed for about a year before moving to Lagan Valley Hospital. Since then he has worked in the Royal Maternity, the Ulster Hospital and is currently working in the Mater Hospital.

In terms of the Muslim community, Dr Hassan tries to participate in most of the activities, arranging and attending celebrations for special occasions such as Eid. He also gives talks on Islam and is taking the children to the Arabic school. In the wider community, he has good relationships with both colleagues and neighbours, participating in Northern Irish celebrations such as New Year and attending social events such as weddings. At work he is a member of the Social Club which organises both educational and social events and he also plays cricket. His boys have good friends from school, whom they play with, both in and outside school and visit each other's homes. Dr Hassan feels it is important to participate actively in the community and socialise.

Thoughts on the future

Dr Hassan believes that the relationship between Muslims and the wider community is very good and there is "a good inter-relationship". He thinks that most of the members of the Muslim community are involved in the wider community either through their profession or through business, which further promotes good relations. For the future, he says:

"I hope for more integration and that the relationship becomes stronger, cemented".

Mrs Nejwa Hassan

Living in Northern Ireland

When Mrs Hassan first came to Northern Ireland things were a little difficult because she did not speak much English, however, once she became more proficient, she began to like living here. She still attends English classes and has now started to learn the computer, going to Lisburn Institute and Al-Nisa.

Before she married, Mrs Hassan was a student and had finished the equivalent of GCSE's. She finds she is busier in Northern Ireland than in Sudan, because there she had a lot of support from her family and the community. In this sense, things are more difficult here. Since moving here, Mrs Hassan says she has made many friends through her classes and in the neighbourhood. She believes she is now much more independent because she needs do things for herself, especially when Dr Hassan is away. She thinks that this experience has been good for her and she now has more confidence, especially now that she can communicate more easily.

Achievements and Contributions

Mrs Hassan is involved in Al-Nisa and attends social events, such as barbecues and trips. She is a member of the Parent Teacher Group at the primary school and supports school events.

Thoughts on the future

Mrs Hassan hopes for good relationships between Muslims and the wider community.

"I would like both communities to help each other, to become more friendly, to have social activities together – to consolidate and unify."

Tariq

Tariq is thirteen and goes to Laurel Hill Community College. He is good at Art, Technology, PE, English and Science, but his favourite subject is Art. Outside school, he likes swimming, tennis and playing the computer. He has just got the results of his exams and says he did "OK" (although his father says he did very well). Of living here he says: "Northern Ireland is very different but it's OK". In the future he would like to be a Plastic Surgeon or a Dentist or start a design business making new products for cars.

Ahmed

Ahmed is ten years old and has just finished Primary 6. He was awarded the Class Trophy in June 2005, because he was good in class. His best subjects are Maths, Science and English, but he particularly enjoys Maths. He also enjoys games, including football and hockey. In the future he would like to be a Lawyer, Footballer or start a business selling parts for engines, like his grandfather. Ahmed can speak some Arabic and goes to the classes at the Northern Ireland Muslim Family Association on Friday and Sunday. Over the summer he hopes to go swimming, to the cinema and play football. His favourite part of school is playing outside and he loves running, recently coming third in the Bean Bag Race at the school Sports Day. He has a lot of friends and one has now moved to America. He keeps in touch with Ahmed by writing and phoning. Ahmed also likes Play Station.

Osama

Osama is seven years old and currently in Primary 3. He is good at multiplying and enjoys Maths. He also enjoys Science and has made salt at school. Like his older brothers, he enjoys sport, particularly running and came first in the school Relay Race. He would like to be a Footballer, a Basketball Player or maybe a Doctor. However, he believes he may be able to fit everything in by being a Basketball Player when he is eighteen and a Footballer when he is twenty, which leaves plenty of time to become a Doctor later.

Mr Jafar A Hasson

Mr Hasson is originally from Iraq and by profession is a Mechanical Engineer. He married while he was studying for his degree at Queen's University and his wife is from Northern Ireland. They have three children, twins who are eleven (a boy and girl) and a boy of ten years old. The family are currently renovating their home and live near Templepatrick.

Living in Northern Ireland

In late 1979, Mr Hasson came to Britain to study English and Technology. He first went to Edinburgh and when he had completed his language studies came to Northern Ireland to study at the University of Ulster, Jordanstown and has been here ever since. He admits that the decision to study in Northern Ireland was purely financial. His father was paying for his courses and studying in Northern Ireland was less expensive than the rest of the UK. However, Mr Hasson found he liked it here, particularly because it was quiet and peaceful. Although he misses home (Iraq) and would love to go back he says he "is living nicely here" and is happy enough. Of his home, he says:

"I think everyone misses their home, but it isn't OK there either".

When he came to Northern Ireland, he shared a house with other people from Iraq, all studying different courses, either at Queen's University or the University of Ulster. He says that, when he came in the early 1980s, there were very few foreign people here and he thinks this was probably due to the 'Troubles'.

Mr Hasson says that he loved the University of Ulster, both the people and the environment. He even enjoyed the journey every morning travelling along the Lough because it was so beautiful. Where he now lives with his family reflects his love of a peaceful environment and the importance of beautiful scenery. He found the weekends as a student could be a bit lonely because there was not much to do, but he made use of this time to work hard for his course. The main problem, he remembers, was in the summer when many of his friends went home. He found that the days were very long and there was little to do, however, whilst at the University of Ulster he did have a work placement, which helped in this respect.

Since Mr Hasson came to Northern Ireland, he has never had any problems here. He thinks that, until recently, people here had their own problems and they did not worry so much about others. This is one of the reasons he stayed, "because it was nice and peaceful and people left you alone". However, he has seen recent changes in the attitude towards people from other countries. He wonders if the ending of the 'Troubles' has given people more time to look around them and they have started to "pick on foreigners". He believes that the media has had a part to play in the more negative attitudes which seem to be developing. But says:

"Thankfully I haven't had any bad experiences and hope I won't have any, people don't really bother".

Achievements and Contributions

Mr Hasson undertook his initial studies in Mechanical Engineering at the University of Ulster, later going to Queen's University to finish his degree. He started work in Shorts Aerospace in 1988 and has now worked there for seventeen years. He is sometimes surprised by this, given the difficulties Shorts has been through in the past, however, it is now enjoying some success.

Mr Hasson is particularly involved in the wider Northern Irish society through his work. He still has many connections with the University of Ulster and sits on the Industrial Advisory Board. At one stage he worked with the Institute of Mechanical Engineering, which promotes engineering in Northern Ireland and also promoted the Institute within Shorts to develop engineering skills there.

His main involvement in the Muslim community is with the Northern Ireland Muslim Family Association, where he takes his children to learn Arabic. It is important for him that his children know Arabic and he also feels it is good for the children to mix with others from different backgrounds.

Thoughts on the future

For the future relationship between the Muslim community and the wider society, Mr Hasson hopes that Muslims will become more integrated within Northern Ireland. Most Muslims he meets are professional people who are involved in the society. He feels particularly that "if you live in a society, the last thing you should do is to isolate yourself", believing that this is wrong. He believes that integration is essential; however, equally essential is keeping one's own principles.

He welcomes the opportunity to interact with those of different faiths and hopes for this to increase in the future.

"That Christians, Jews and Muslims all get together but everyone keeps their own principals – everyone respects everyone else – that is what I'm hopeful for – just that all this trouble and hassle will disappear, in Northern Ireland especially".

He also hopes for peace in Northern Ireland, especially for his children's sake. He finds it upsetting to witness the behaviour of some young people, damaging things and getting drunk, for instance, the problems in the 'Holy Lands' in Belfast earlier in 2005. He sees it as a waste of money, time and effort as well as of Police resources. He says:

"You don't live your life to waste it like that. You're here to work and enjoy it – give something and take what you need".

Mr Hasson was very upset by the explosions in London on 7/7. He hopes that we will learn from it that there are people who are "terrorist by nature". He points out that they are not only terrorising Christians or the Jewish, but are terrorising everybody, all human beings, calling them "criminals against human beings". He hopes that everybody will see that and not judge all Muslims as the same.

Dr Zamir and Mrs Iffat Huda

Dr Huda is originally from Pakistan and has been in the UK since 1971, initially in Glasgow. He is married to Iffat, who is also from Pakistan and they have a daughter and two sons. Their daughter studied Medicine and is now a Consultant Psychiatrist; their oldest son went to Imperial College, London and graduated in Maths and Management and then Law. He is now a Corporate Finance Lawyer in the City of London. Their youngest son, who was born in Dundonald, completed a BSc in Maths and Economics and an MSc in Computers at Queen's University. He has been working for the Red Cross in London for the past two years.

Living in Northern Ireland

Dr Huda was living and working in Glasgow when he applied for a post in Enniskillen. He says:

"The administrative officer in Enniskillen talked to me for half an hour on the phone, just to come and look at the place so I came and looked at the place. She gave me a cottage on the shore of Lough Erne. You couldn't ask for anything more than that so ... I didn't go to any other interviews, forgot about everything else and settled in Northern Ireland".

He moved to Enniskillen 1973 and then to Dungannon in 1974. For him, one of the main reasons for deciding to move to Northern Ireland was that the people were so nice and friendly. He has now been here for over thirty years. All his children were brought up here and the family have made many good friends within the local community.

Neither Dr Huda nor his family have ever experienced any difficulties in Northern Ireland. However, other members of the Muslim community in this region have had some problems. These have occurred mainly in Portadown and were orchestrated, he believes, by people who came to Northern Ireland from other parts of the UK. The British National Party, in particular, have leafleted in the area, stirring up resentment.

Most of the problems seemed to start when an application was made to build an Islamic Centre in Craigavon. Planning Permission had been granted to build it on land which was donated by a member of the Muslim community, however, this was in a very sensitive area and quite isolated. A campaign against the building was started and this increased local tensions. The events around the proposal and the campaign against it were reported last year in a documentary produced by Newsnight for which Dr Huda was interviewed. In the end, it was felt there was no point in going ahead without the approval and consent of local people because of the likelihood of vandalism and the possibility that local Muslims would be victimised. It was, therefore, decided to postpone the project until a suitable alternative was found.

Achievements and Contributions

Dr Huda qualified in Medicine in 1963. Between 1971 and 1973 he was working in paediatrics in Glasgow and had planned to specialise in this. However, he found this was not possible at that time in Northern Ireland, so he moved into medicine and planned to specialise as a physician. Whilst in the hospital, he had several offers of work as a Consultant Paediatrician outside the UK but decided to remain here. In 1977, his post in Enniskillen ended and he had to decide whether he would stay in Northern Ireland or move. An important consideration was his children's education and the excellence of the schools in the area was a deciding factor. The decision to remain in Northern Ireland, prompted Dr Huda to go into General Practice and he remained a GP until his retirement in 1997. His retirement was prompted by two heart attacks which were partly due to the stress and pressure of General Practice work. Since retiring he has been doing private work, including acupuncture and hypnotherapy. He says that he is probably busier than before, but the work is less stressful and he is no longer 'on call'.

In his professional role, Dr Huda was the Chairman of the Northern Ireland Division of the Overseas Doctors Association in the UK for about ten years. At the Annual General Meeting in 1995, which was held in Northern Ireland, he was made a Fellow of the Association.

When he first came here, there were very few Muslims and meetings were held in each other's houses. The community then bought a house in Eglantine Avenue, eventually selling it to build the Belfast Islamic Centre (BIC) and Mosque in Wellington Park. Dr Huda was one of the founder members of BIC and a Trustee for several years. Sadly, there are very few of the founder members still involved in BIC and he resigned a few years ago because of political differences.

For the past two years he has been involved in the Craigavon Islamic Centre and is one of the Trustees. In particular, he has offered his expertise to advise the group about building an Islamic Centre for this region. He has also been leading the Friday prayers for the past two years. A teacher has now been appointed to take classes for the children and also now leads the Friday prayer. Currently the community are using a local hall but would like to build their own centre, to have a place of their own.

Thoughts on the future

Dr Huda's ambition is for the Muslim community to build a proper Islamic Centre in Craigavon and to employ a full-time teacher for the children. The latter is important because few people have the time to teach their children about Islam at home and it is not usually included in Religious Education in schools. The centre would be used for prayer but also would allow people to visit and learn about Islam. He feels that there is not much awareness of other religions in Northern Ireland and, consequently, people are overly influenced by how they see Islam portrayed in the media. Dr Huda points out that Islam literally means peace and submission and that it is a peaceful religion, but believes that this is not known in the wider community. He feels that it is unfair that, although Muslims have lived in Northern Ireland for many years and are part of this society, they have not been allowed to have their own place to pray in the local area. In the Newsnight documentary, he asked of a local councillor:

"We have been here for twenty, thirty, forty years, have we not the right to pray in our own place, somewhere in the Craigavon area? Why should we go to Belfast or Dublin to pray – would you like to go to Dublin or Belfast for your Sunday prayers".

He says "we don't want to confront anyone, we just want to live in harmony and peace but we have the right to pray in our own place". He points to the size of the Muslim community in Craigavon, which numbers between three and four hundred adults, plus children and how it is unreasonable to try to deny a group this size their own centre. Despite the recent setbacks, Dr Huda is confident that it is just a matter of time before an Islamic Centre will be built in the area.

Mrs Iffat Huda

Mrs Huda is a Microbiologist by training. She has almost completed her Counselling training and is very involved in charity work. She has volunteered for the Samaritans, the National Society for the Prevention of Cruelty to Children (NSPCC) and the Parent and Children Group. Mrs Huda designed the family garden and five years ago it won first prize for the Shamrock All Ireland Garden Competition. The garden has been opened for the National Trust twice and is going to be opened again this year. Five years ago she raised £6,000 for Marie Curie, NSPCC and the Samaritans through organising tea stalls during the open day.

Misses Dana, Noor & Hibba Jaber

Dana

Dana's parents are originally from Palestine and she was born in Kuwait. She moved to the UK in 1993, when she was six and she is now eighteen.

Living in Northern Ireland

The family first lived in Newcastle, Co.Down for eight years and moved to Belfast when Dana was fourteen. It was difficult living in Belfast at first because where they lived in Newcastle was much quieter, however, Dana liked the school she went to and that helped her to get used to living here.

Dana says that dealing with stereotypes and prejudice can be difficult, but that living in Northern Ireland has been mostly positive and she has not experienced any racism at either of her schools. However, she believes racism is increasing here and she has experienced it where she lives and so have some of her friends. She feels that mixing with people in school and people wanting to know about Islam has been positive, as has been the recognition she has been given for her academic achievements.

Achievements and Contributions

Dana did well at school and achieved GCSE's in Arabic, French, History, German, Information Technology, Science, Maths, English and Religious Education. She has just finished her 'A' levels in French, English Literature, Information Technology, Arabic, History and plans to go to Queen's University to study Law and French. She is particularly interested in Human Rights Law.

She won the 'All Children Together Award' (the Millennium Award for enhancing the culture and ethos of integration) 2003-2004, for her contribution to integration at her school, Lagan College. It involved being part of the Justice Group at school, debating issues in class and representing the school outside. As part of the Justice Group she gave talks about the different celebrations in Islam. The purpose was mainly to raise awareness and tell people about Islam. This, she feels, helps to stop people stereotyping Muslims. She has also taken part in radio interviews and was interviewed for a Save the Children publication. She did her work experience at the Northern Ireland Council for Ethnic Minorities (NICEM). Because she wants to be a lawyer, she worked in the Racial Harassment Project and also translated materials into Arabic. She was involved in the 'Make Poverty History' Campaign and took part in a protest outside the City Hall with the Lord Mayor. Last year she raised money for the Samaritans.

Dana is an active member of Al-Nisa and the Northern Ireland Muslim Family Association (NIMFA) and is a member of the youth groups of both organisations. The youth groups are planning cross community projects with churches, but mainly they offer classes for the members such as Arabic and Religious Studies, as well as discussions on issues which affect young Muslims here. Dana believes her activities show that, as a Muslim, she can still contribute to society.

Thoughts on the future

She would like to see the Muslim community expand and, for Northern Ireland as a whole, she would like to see people from different religions and different cultural backgrounds unite to fight prejudice and stereotypes and raise awareness.

Noor

Noor is fourteen years old and was born in Jordan. She moved to Northern Ireland when she was ten years old.

Living in Northern Ireland

She originally moved to Newcastle-upon-Tyne when she was two years old and, initially, did not want to move to Belfast, preferring to stay in her old school. However, when she moved here she found she liked the school and she made "lots of new friends". She is now at Lagan College, which she enjoys, her favourite subjects being French and History. Even though she was the only person from Carryduff Primary School to go there she was able, again, to make plenty of new friends.

She finds there are sometimes difficulties for young Muslims here, for example, sometimes people call them names. She feels it is good to get to know other people from different backgrounds and religions and people mixing together. She believes it is easier to mix with other people when you are younger, because of school. She feels that "this is good, because you grow up knowing about your own religion and other peoples and make friends with other people as well as Muslims".

Achievements and Contributions

Noor was presented with an award for academic achievement in year nine, a certificate for coming third in Lagan College Enterprise Education Competition and a medal for coming first in netball in the Northern Ireland League, 2004. She also got a certificate for taking part in NICEM's consultation on the Children & Young People's Strategy.

She is good at sport, enjoying netball, hockey, tennis and gymnastics. In October 2005, she will be a member of a netball team going on a tour of Spain and is a member of the hockey team at school, playing in the right wing position.

In September 2005 she plans to start an anti-racism club at school with some of her friends. They will discuss the problems and issues relating to racism and organise activities. Other pupils will be able to join and its aim is to make things better in school and outside.

She would like to be either a Vet working with pets, because she likes animals or a Psychiatrist, because she thinks it would be interesting. She has liked animals since she was very small and has a pet cat. She is studying Geography, ICT, French, Double Award Science (Biology, Chemistry & Physics) for GCSE's and has History for her reserve. Noor feels she is good at communicating. At the end of next year she will be going on work placement and thinks she may work with animals.

Noor is a member of Al-Nisa's and NIMFA's Young Peoples Groups. She goes to NIMFA on a Friday night and Sunday morning where she learns Arabic and Islamic Studies and does arts and crafts.

Thoughts on the future

In terms of the future, Noor would like people to respect Muslims more and for more Muslims to live here. She feels it is more difficult being part of a very small group because "if there are more people you feel freer and other people won't do what they do if there is a bigger group".

Hibba

Hibba was born in Northern Ireland and is eight years old. She goes to Carryduff Primary School and is going into Primary 5 in September, 2005. She is looking forward to this because she will start swimming then. She feels being the youngest is good because she doesn't have to help in the house yet.

Achievements and Contributions

Hibba's favourite subjects at school are Maths, English, PE, Art, History and Geography and she is very good at Art. On Thursdays she does art and crafts and takes part in Athletics Clubs. She likes athletics best and is good at PE, especially bench ball. She likes school because she can meet all her friends there.

She is learning Arabic and also about Islam at NIMFA and goes on holiday to Jordan and Palestine.

Mrs Sonbol Khalili

Mrs Khalili is originally from Tehran, Iran. She lives in Lisburn and is married with one daughter who is seventeen. Her daughter is still at school and is doing her 'A' levels.

Living in Northern Ireland

The decision to settle in Northern Ireland was made after Mrs Khalili came to here to visit her brother for a holiday. He had been here for twenty-seven years and she decided to stay because she wanted to study Hairdressing. Mrs Khalili has now been in Northern Ireland for eleven years, first living in Belfast and later moving to Lisburn. She says that she liked it here: "because it was quiet and nice".

When moving to another country, the attitudes of the people from there are particularly important and determine how well a person settles. She says she loves Northern Ireland because she has found the people here to be very kind and friendly, saying:

"It is very important when you move to a different country that people are nice to you".

Being away from your home could, she feels, lead to depression; however, meeting other people can help make things easier. When she first arrived, she did not feel very comfortable because she could not speak any English. However, she very soon started to attend English classes, firstly at the Multi-Cultural Resource Centre (MCRC) and then Belfast Institute and through these was able to meet people. Mrs Khalili particularly enjoys the opportunity to meet people from diverse backgrounds. The classes she attended enabled her to do this and to socialise with people outside her immediate circle. Her involvement in the Muslim community has also enabled her to meet people from different countries and cultures. She says: "we are all Muslims but because we are from different countries we have different cultures – this is nice to have". Mrs Khalili counts people from many different countries and cultures as her friends here.

Once Mrs Khalili had learnt English, things became easier for her. Living away from her family has, she believes, made her stronger. In Iran she had her family to help and support her, but here she has had to solve her own problems and do things for herself. Her ability to cope and succeed in a new country has, she says, given her much more confidence in her own abilities.

Mrs Khalili says she has not had any difficulties living as a Muslim in Northern Ireland, but feels things are better now there are organisations such as Al-Nisa.

Achievements and Contributions

Before coming to Northern Ireland, Mrs Khalili trained as a Hairdresser in Iran and also worked in this area. She wanted to do further training here and once she had learnt English, completed her Level II in Hairdressing at Belfast Institute and her Level III at Lisburn Institute. However, she has not worked in Northern Ireland, except during the two years she was training, when she had a work placement as part of her course.

She has been a member of Al-Nisa for nearly two years and involves herself in their activities, for example, the social events and educational courses. She also values the opportunity Al-Nisa offers to just talk to other women. It is a very important part of Mrs Khalili's life and is, she says: "like a second home". Al-Nisa, she says, also plays an important role in teaching children about Muslim culture and Islam. She says: "life changes and we have to move with it but we also have to keep our culture".

Thoughts on the future

For the future, Mrs Khalili hopes that different cultures and religions will mix more: "we all believe in God – we should be a lot closer". For her, having different beliefs should not stop people being friends. In Tehran, she says, she was used to people living together from different countries and having different religions and would like this to happen in Northern Ireland.

"I would like everyone to understand each other – it is very important in life. We only live for a certain time and it is better to be friends and keep good company and help each other – it makes an easy life. I have always felt like that".

Mrs Amtul Salam Khan

Mrs Khan is originally from Pakistan and came to Northern Ireland in January 1986 when she married Dr Mazhar Khan. By profession she is a Nurse, however, since coming to Northern Ireland, has been active in the voluntary sector, particularly in her role of setting up Al-Nisa. She was kept very busy over the years bringing up "three lovely boys and is now enjoying the company of three very caring daughters in-law and six precious grandchildren".

Living in Northern Ireland

Mrs Khan had always previously lived in hot countries, so her first impression of Northern Ireland was that it was very cold. Her husband had told her to wear something warm but in her experience, that just meant a light jumper. She has always preferred cool weather but did not expect such a low temperature. People in Northern Ireland, she found, were very friendly and extremely helpful. Her first close association was with the wife of a colleague of her husband, called Ruth. She gave her "precious time" to help Mrs Khan become familiar with the various systems for everyday life in Northern Ireland. She also helped her to learn and practice driving.

The 'Troubles' were still fairly serious when Mrs Khan first came here but they did not affect her directly and she was not particularly worried about living here, in her own words she says: "all countries have their problems". She narrates her experience of being ushered through security checks without being searched. Mrs Khan says that she has never experienced any racism here and made friends very quickly. She has generally found people here warm and approachable.

For Mrs Khan, Northern Ireland is her home and she wants to spend the rest of her life here.

Achievements and Contributions

As a Nurse, Mrs Khan worked in both Pakistan and Saudi Arabia. She trained for three years in General Nursing and then undertook a further year in Midwifery. She chose nursing rather than teaching, as a career, because she felt it was a very practical way to help people. Whilst still in her twenties, Mrs Khan was promoted to Deputy Matron in her hospital in Pakistan and was recruited as a Staff Nurse for the hospital in Saudi Arabia. Within a year of being there, she had been promoted to shift leader and then later to Ward Sister, also receiving the 'Best Nurse Award'. The hospital in Saudi Arabia was staffed by people from many different countries, so she needed good communication skills and awareness of diversity in order to be able to work there.

Since coming to Northern Ireland, Mrs Khan has participated in various training courses, including: Community Interpreting; Training the Trainers and Diversity and Equality Training; Computer Skills; Foundation in Counselling; First Aid; Personal Development; Religious Diversity and Pre-registration for Childminders. She is a registered tutor with the Workers Educational Association and Queen's University, delivering seminars on Islamic culture and tradition. She also conducts an information session for new recruits in the PSNI.

Since she had worked up until she was married, Mrs Khan realised very early on that she needed to be active, even if she was not in paid employment. Soon after arriving here she became aware of the need for a suitable place for Muslim women to get together. She learnt to drive, passing her test in 1987, and this gave her the freedom to start working in an informal and voluntary way with other Muslim women, offering both practical and emotional support to those in need. Within two years Mrs Khan had joined the Belfast Islamic Centre (BIC), and set up an informal women's group. This started by offering classes in Islamic education and Halaqa, (which literally means study circle). A few years later she became the teacher liaison volunteer with the children's Sunday School at BIC. The women's group came together through the classes and, in 1992, Mrs Khan was co-opted onto the Executive Committee of BIC, as the women's representative. Her role was to inform the Executive Committee of the needs of Muslim women and their problems.

Realising that the language barrier could mean women were very isolated, language classes were another innovation which the group initiated. An arrangement with Belfast Institute for Further and Higher Education put the classes on a more formal setting. Mrs Khan also taught Islamic Studies, which was her main area of interest at school and college, in both Urdu and English.

The group formally became the Women's Group (BIC) in 1998 and had its first Annual General Meeting, continuing its affiliation with BIC until 2001.

At the end of 2001, Al-Nisa decided to become a completely independent organisation, became a registered charity and moved out of BIC premises. The years between the first informal group and the official launch of Al-Nisa were important in that they laid the ground work which made an independent group possible. As Mrs Khan says:

"In my mind, since I came here, I saw a need for a group to support women, to be a voice, to support their human rights."

Al-Nisa started the year 2002 with no premises and no funds, so used Mrs Khan's house to meet. However, the Equality Commission and a number of voluntary sector organisations, such as, the Northern Ireland Council for Ethnic Minorities (NICEM), the Multi-Cultural Resource Centre (MCRC) and the Women's Support Network were supportive of Al-Nisa, recognising the valuable contribution of their work. The Women's Support Network investigated possible premises and, eventually, Women's Aid offered a house they no longer used. In May 2002, Al-Nisa held an open day for its members, which had a very good turnout and in August 2002, arranged another, this time inviting organisations from across the voluntary and public sector. Of the fifty three which were invited, fifty one attended. At this event, Dame Joan Harbinson, from the Equality Commission, gave a very positive and supportive speech. A number of funders attended the open day and afterwards, Al-Nisa made an appeal for help to find premises. Through this, in early 2002, Al-Nisa secured a grant from the OFMDFM and this award enabled them to rent their current house in Stranmillis. Al-Nisa is still funded by OFMDFM, under the core funding grant programme for black and minority ethnic organisations, but now also receives funding from Belfast City Council and from other funders for specific projects.

With more financial security for the group, Mrs Khan has now had the opportunity to contemplate the hard work and struggles she endured in setting up Al-Nisa. She had to face strong opposition and personal attacks, because some members of the community did not approve of Al-Nisa and tried to create obstructions. It was essentially her personal commitment and drive which made it possible for her to continue, along with the support of a core group of members. She has devoted her life, since coming to Northern Ireland, to benefit the Muslim community, particularly through her work with Muslim women. The challenges were worthwhile because this important and active group now provides a platform for the voices of Muslim women. However, Mrs Khan does not want to accept that it is she who has achieved this but rather, that it is through the power of prayer: "No matter what we achieve, it is the will of Allah". (God)

Mrs Khan sees her work with Al-Nisa as being concerned with trying to break down barriers by raising awareness and by working with Muslim women to overcome those barriers. She believes the key to the group's success was its commitment to training the Management Committee which ensured appropriate policies and procedures were put in place. Her husband, Dr. Khan, however, believes it is through her endless enthusiasm.

Mrs Khan's community activity has been recognised in a number of ways. In 2003, for example, she was presented with the 'Outstanding Contribution' Award at NICEM's Volunteer of the Year Award and the Voluntary Services Bureau 'Volunteer Achievement Award'. Finally, in June 2004, Mrs Khan received an MBE, in recognition of her overall contribution towards Muslim women in Northern Ireland.

Through her involvement with Al-Nisa and independently, Mrs Khan has spoken at several conferences, including: the Visible Women's Conference, 2001; the Business and Professional Women's Association and the PSNI Conference. She is also a member of a range of committees within the voluntary and public sectors. In terms of minority ethnic organisations, she was on the Board of Director's of both NICEM from 1999 to 2003 and MCRC between 1998 and 2004, being Vice Chairperson of NICEM between 2001 and 2003. She is currently the representative for black and minority ethnic communities on the Board of Directors of Highway to Health. Furthermore, she is a member of: the Multi-Cultural Independent Advisory Group of PSNI; the Minority Ethnic Equality Forum of the Equality Commission for Northern Ireland and the Racial Equality Forum of OFMDFM, being also a member of its thematic sub-group on Languages. She has also participated in numerous consultation processes and reports designed to improve services. In all these roles she represents the views of the Muslim community in general and Muslim women specifically.

Mrs Khan has produced a number of publications on behalf of Al-Nisa. These include: the *Muslim Culture and Traditions Information Pack* and fact sheets on Muslim culture for the Health Service, Education Department, Social Services and the PSNI. The pack was nominated for 'Idea of the Year' by Community Change. She was also involved in the production of leaflets, audio and video tapes called 'First Steps in Health Care Services in Northern Ireland' for the South and East Belfast Trust.

In terms of the media, Mrs Khan set up Al-Nisa's UTV community service announcement, has taken part in the BBC's Faces of Islam programme (UK Islam season) and has given numerous interviews to newspapers. In addition she undertakes interpreting and translation work and gives talks on Islam and the Muslim community. Finally, she is also involved in Belfast's Annual Food Festival and other multi-cultural events.

Thoughts on the future

Mrs Khan is a very positive person and can see a very bright future for Northern Ireland. However, she acknowledges there are serious issues which need to be addressed. She says equality is not just about multi-culturalism, sharing food, hosting cultural events or a talking shop. These responses can avoid the real problem and ignore the needs of the minority ethnic communities in Northern Ireland. She believes that after 9/11 and 7/7, people need to sit down and find a solution, but first they need to discover the roots of the problem. This needs to be done without resorting to denial and blame and by recognising that there will not just be one cause. Responsibility cannot be laid solely with either the Muslim community or the British Government. Consideration must be given to all aspects, including community, environment, media and governmental foreign policy. She does not believe that the problems are insoluble and says that all that is needed is real commitment. To solve these problems is essential because, as she says, "we should not allow anyone to destroy the peacefulness of this country".

In this regard one of her favourite quotes is by Albert Camus,

"Don't walk behind me, I may not lead. Don't walk in front of me, I may not follow. Just walk beside me and be my friend." (attributed to Albert Camus 1913-1960, www.quotationspage.com)

Mrs Khan believes all her successes came from Allah (God), but she would also like to thank her family, particularly her husband and Muslim and non-Muslim friends, particularly Nazneen Raza and Gabrielle Doherty.

Dr Mazhar Khan

Dr Khan was born in India but moved to Pakistan after partition. He lives in Belfast and is married to Amtul Salam Khan, who is well known for "her pioneering work in setting up a very vibrant Muslim Women's organisation" (see separate entry). They have three sons who were all educated at Methodist College, Belfast. None of them followed their father's profession, despite achieving very good grades in their 'A' level examinations. Their eldest son, Ashar, studied Computer Science at the University of York, joining Andersen Management Consultants after graduation. He is currently working as a Senior Manager for the company, which is now known as ACCENTURE. Their second son, Badar, graduated in Engineering Management from the University of Brunel. He later completed a Masters of Business Administration at Wharton Business School, University of Pennsylvania. He is currently working as Vice President for British Gas/ Centrica in the USA. Their youngest son, Mubashir, joined British Airways after graduating in Aeronautical Engineering, from the University of Southampton. He is now a Senior Flight Officer with this company. Their children are now all married and their wives are all law graduates. Dr and Mrs Khan have six grandchildren.

Living in Northern Ireland

Dr Khan came to Northern Ireland in 1978 for a job interview. It was just after the La Mon House bomb and he was so nervous he sat in a cinema for three hours while he waited for the bus to take him back to the airport.

Despite his initial reservations regarding the 'Troubles', Dr Khan has found his time in Northern Ireland "extremely pleasant". He found people on both sides of the community very friendly and he has never been shown any disrespect; indeed, he feels he has been treated with great affection.

Dr Khan chose Northern Ireland because he wanted experience with mobile cardiac care units. The first unit in the world was used in Northern Ireland and they seemed to work better here than elsewhere. The success of these units was based on two things; a high degree of focus and asking the right questions before deployment. The model developed here was transferred to the US, other regions of the UK, Europe and Australia.

One particular incident opened Dr Khan's eyes to the situation in Belfast soon after his arrival. He was called to a Shankill Pub where a customer had suffered a cardiac arrest. After examining him, Dr Khan realised the man would not survive. Another man, who was 'half drunk', asked if there was anything he could do and Dr Khan asked him to "call a priest". This comment nearly caused a riot. The next time he made sure to ask someone who he should send for and made himself familiar with the demography of Belfast very quickly.

Achievements and Contributions

Dr Khan qualified in Medicine from King Edward Medical College, Lahore, in 1962. Following his initial training, he then continued his postgraduate training in Vienna, followed by his MRCP (by examination) at the Royal College of Physicians in London. He continued his training in Birmingham, Liverpool and Belfast and became a Fellow of Royal College of Physicians, London.

Professor Pantridge, a Consultant at the Royal Victoria Hospital, invited Dr Khan to Northern Ireland to take up the post of Senior Registrar in Cardiology in his department. In 1980, Dr Khan went to Saudi Arabia as a Consultant, returning to Northern Ireland in 1982 to take over the position of Consultant Cardiologist, vacated by the retirement of Professor Pantridge. Prior to his formal retirement, he was the Director of the Cardiac Catheterization Unit at the Royal. He would now describe himself as semi-retired and works for the Royal and Mater Hospitals as a part-time Consultant three days a week.

Dr Khan has led the development in a number of areas in cardiology. He performed the first angioplasty in Northern Ireland in 1982 and developed a guide catheter designed for undertaking right coronary interventions with 'stents'. Dr Khan pioneered the use of Implantable Cardioverter Defibrillators and, in 1990, he implanted the first of these in Ireland. He also pioneered the "technique of coated 'stents' with an anti-rejection drug to prevent clogging of heart arteries" and is now developing a new type of 'stent'. His future plans include the launch, in United States of America (after a successful introduction in Paris in May 2005), of a "revolutionary guide catheter" which he has designed.

Training, education and development within the medical field are of central concern for Dr Khan and he is currently overseeing a "virtual reality system of surgery to train doctors". He was a founding member of the British Cardiovascular Intervention Society and has also been a member of several cardiology working groups at European level. Finally, he has been published widely in medical journals and contributed chapters to several books.

Dr Khan played cricket for his university and continued to play for the Royal Victoria team. He is now an Honorary Member of Irvinestown Cricket Club. His other interests include classical music and he regularly attends performances of the Ulster Orchestra.

In terms of the Muslim community, Dr Khan's involvement has included being the Vice-President of the Belfast Islamic Centre (BIC) between 1985 & 1987 and the President between 1987 & 1989. He was responsible for purchasing the current premises, which can hold up to one hundred and forty people for prayers. The building cost £58,000 to buy and a further £20,000 was spent on refurbishment. Funds were raised to purchase and refurbish the current premises through certifying meat as halal and other voluntary collections. The BIC had a very important role in the mid 1980s in ensuring halal meat was properly produced and providing certification of the meat. The certification stopped in 1989 because of BIC's inability to vouch that the meat was appropriately slaughtered. Dr Khan became a Trustee of BIC in 1992 and held this position until 2003. He is currently researching the history of Muslims in Ireland with a view to publishing a book. Part of his research forms the first section of this book.

Hopes for the Future

Dr Khan believes there is a need for greater understanding of the Muslim community by the majority community and believes that many people are still unaware of Muslim culture and traditions. He suggests that a Department could be set up in Queen's University to study the faiths of Abraham - to find common understandings. He also feels that, within the school system, Religious Education should be broadened to look at comparative religions, with experts from different religions giving input. This would, in some measure, counteract the negative portrayal of Islam which is prevalent in the Western media. There is, he believes, a paucity of correct information about Islam outside Mosques and there is a need to present a more balanced view. Where crimes are committed, for example, terrorist crimes, those who commit them should not be referred to in religious terms, since crimes should not be given a religious label.

Ms Pakeeza Khan

Originally from Pakistan, Ms Khan also lived in Kuwait before moving to Northern Ireland in 1990. She has two adult children, Rafay and Ghazal, who have also been interviewed. By profession she is a Journalist and currently works as an Administration Officer. She lives in Warrenpoint with her son, who has just finished university.

Living in Northern Ireland

Ms Khan moved to Northern Ireland during the Gulf War when her former husband was offered a job in Newry. When they moved, her daughter was eleven years old and her son was seven. After Kuwait was liberated in 1991, Ms Khan decided to stay in Northern Ireland rather than returning there. One of the main reasons she had for this decision was the high standard of education here. She says:

"in hindsight, I made a wise decision from which both my children have benefited and their success is my dream realised. Northern Ireland is our home and we are very happy here".

Of living in Northern Ireland, Ms Khan says that she and her children have friends from both of the main communities and her friends and colleagues have "come to understand and respect the moderately liberal Muslim lifestyle that my children and I lead". She feels that her background has not been a barrier and there is a genuine interest in her culture which reflects a desire to learn about other ways of life. Her experience in Warrenpoint and Newry contrasts with the "hostile attitudes" reported in areas of Belfast. Ms Khan believes that she is generally treated with the same respect as everyone else and that the relationship with her friends has led to a mutual benefit and growth:

"the dignity and festivity so characteristic of my culture is something that ... has enriched their lives, as their ways have done mine".

Ms Khan has had mainly positive experiences of living in Northern Ireland. She has found that people here are "generally open minded and easy to mesh with".

Achievements and Contributions

Ms Khan has a Master's Degree in Journalism and during 1970 and 1980 worked in radio and television broadcasting, as well as writing for newspapers and magazines in both Pakistan and Kuwait. Since 1995 she has been working as an Administration Officer in various companies in the Newry/Warrenpoint area. She says that, since she became a lone parent in 1994, she has worked "as hard as was humanly possible" to bring up her two children single handed, without the additional support of family. She is proud of the achievements of her two children, academically, professionally and personally.

Thoughts on the future

The relationship between Muslims and the wider community has not been an issue which Ms Khan had given much consideration to until recently. However, in the light of recent world events, Ms Khan hopes:

"that people in Northern Ireland will remain open-minded and willing to objectively understand Muslim beliefs and lifestyles which, in their uncorrupted form, are quite liberal and progressive, contrary to common perceptions".

Mrs Ghazal Khan-Cunningham

Mrs Khan-Cunningham was born in Kuwait, although her parents were originally from Pakistan and she lived there until she was eleven. By profession, she is a Magazine Editor and Publisher and is married to Fin Cunningham, who is a Journalist. She was brought up in Warrenpoint, where her mother and brother still live and now lives in Carlingford.

Living in Northern Ireland

The family left Kuwait during the Gulf War, settling in Northern Ireland when Mrs Khan-Cunningham's father started working for an engineering firm in Newry. She says she never felt she was defined by her religion by any of her "peers, teachers, friends or colleagues". Although she thinks this may be partly because she does not "wear" her background or religion as a symbol of who she is and also because she is "fortunate enough to be surrounded by well travelled, educated and broad minded people".

Mrs Khan-Cunningham would say that she has the same liberal outlook and approach to things as her Irish friends and colleagues. She believes that people are largely open to learning about her background and do not appear to see it as something that makes her socially inaccessible. She cannot think of any instances where she might have been discriminated against. Indeed, Mrs Khan-Cunningham has reached an advanced stage in her profession much sooner than others her age, showing that religion has not proven to be a factor that has held her back in any way.

Achievements and Contributions

Graduating with a BA Degree in Law from Queen's University, she worked as a Journalist at a publishing company for two years, before joining Accent Magazines, Ltd. She is one of three Directors of this company and Editor of the main title.

Friends are drawn from both the Muslim and local communities, although she is not involved in any community events, as such. She says it is rare for her to attend the Islamic Centre in Belfast as her family have quite a liberal approach to religion and attending prayers is not part of their routine or lifestyle. For Mrs Khan-Cunningham, lifestyle and beliefs are a personal choice, saying:

"I don't necessarily feel the need to commune with others in the context of worship in order to maintain my identity".

Thoughts on the future

Although Mrs Khan-Cunningham has had a positive experience of living in Northern Ireland, she is aware that others have not. She is concerned about the potential for a social backlash against minorities in general, in light of world events since 9/11.

"I know that some degree of heterophobia will always exist in most societies, especially in areas where people live in poor socio-economic conditions and social divisions are more common".

She hopes, however, that Northern Ireland will continue to embrace people of other ethnicities, and that Muslims will not be defined by the approach of small groups who choose to present their political protests under the guise of a religious crusade.

Mrs Khan-Cunningham believes that:

"People of different ethnicities and religious beliefs can only co-exist happily in a progressive society and in order for Northern Ireland to be truly progressive, all sides – indigenous and minorities – have to become a little less rigid and a little more objective in their attitudes towards different lifestyles".

She has found that being invited to join as a guest in alternative festivities and traditions always seems to bond people closer together. Mrs Khan-Cunningham believes that:

"Northern Ireland can be a refreshing and cosmopolitan society if people of all religious backgrounds are gracious enough to honour each other's lifestyles by celebrating them equally and maybe even borrowing good examples from other ways of life".

Mr Louay Majeed & Mrs Thelfa Ahmad

Mr Majeed is originally from Iraq and is a Businessman. He came to the UK in 1984 and moved to Northern Ireland in 1987. In 1997 he married Thelfa, who is also from Iraq. They have four children, three girls and a boy: their two elder daughters are Zehra, who is seven years old and Tesneem, who is five. Their youngest boy and girl are twins called Abdullah and Noor, respectively and they are three years old. The family live in the Newtownbreda area of Belfast.

Living in Northern Ireland

The reason Mr Majeed came to the UK was to receive medical treatment. While he was undergoing treatment he decided to use his time well and started to do his 'O' and 'A' levels. He was initially in London for a year and then Newcastle-upon-Tyne for two years. He came to Northern Ireland after completing his 'A' levels to study Electronics and Computer Hardware at the University of Ulster.

This period was quite difficult because he lived in the halls of residence. He found it could be lonely at weekends, because most students went home and social events focussed on the bar. However, Mr Majeed is certain that his beliefs helped him through this period and the experience made him stronger. He felt that, when he first came to Northern Ireland, things were a bit more difficult for Muslims. Things have become easier, though, as the community has grown, especially now there are centres where Muslims can meet and pray. Mr Majeed feels Northern Ireland is a good place to live and bring up a family.

Achievements and Contributions

On completing his degree, Mr Majeed worked as an Electronic Engineer for Nortel in Monkstown and then at Daewoo. He became self-employed in 1993 when he opened his first restaurant, opening his second one in Botanic Avenue a couple of years later. As well as running his various businesses, which now also include property development, Mr Majeed is active in the Northern Ireland Muslim Family Association (NIMFA), being a member of the Executive Committee. He is also completing his Master's Degree in Electronics at Queen's University.

Thoughts on the future

Mr Majeed would like there to be more facilities where Muslims can meet. He believes that Muslims make a substantial contribution to Northern Irish society and would like the wider community to be aware of this. He wants his children to be integrated into the society here, but also feels it is important for them to maintain their own culture, religion and identity.

Mrs Thelfa Ahmed Majeed

Mrs Majeed completed a degree in Iraq and, since coming to Northern Ireland, has also studied English and Information Technology. She does not work, being a full-time wife and mother, but does volunteer with NIMFA, teaching Arabic to the children of members. Their children all attend local primary schools.

Mrs Majeed feels that people here are very friendly but thinks they are maybe not very aware of Muslim beliefs and culture. An example she gave was of a neighbour who believed that she wore hijab all the time, even in front of her husband.

Hassan Mansour

Although Hassan is from Jordan, his mother is Syrian and his father was a Sherkes, one of the Muslims of Russia who moved to the Middle East after the Russian Revolution. His mother is still alive but his father died in 1994. He was educated at a French school in Bethlehem and at sixteen left school and home, moving to Kuwait to live with his aunt. During this time, he worked in various occupations, including photography, banking and translating.

Whilst based in Kuwait, he travelled to Germany on holiday and, from there he hitchhiked around Europe. On the way back, he visited his parents who persuaded him to return to Jordan. While there, he made several friends within the international community and, because of his travels in Europe, was asked by the mother of one of his English friends to drive the family to Britain. In 1973 he left for England where, after a few months, he found work as a musician.

Hassan has been married for almost thirty-two years and his wife is from Northern Ireland. They have two sons and also grandchildren, the oldest being seven. His younger son lives here and his older son is in Canada. Hassan and his wife live with her mother, who is almost ninety years old. They chose to live with her because she now suffers from ill health and his wife cares for her full-time.

Although born a Muslim, it was not until his father-in-law died in 1990 that Hassan started to practice in a serious way. It was Ramadan and he started praying and fasting. He says he had a lot to learn because he had not had an Islamic upbringing and had attended a Catholic school.

Living in Northern Ireland

Hassan came to Northern Ireland in 1973 to play drums for a soul singer who had a contract to perform at the Abercorn in Belfast for a week. He met his wife the first night they were here and they were married a month later.

Hassan and his wife have lived in London, Northern Ireland and the Middle East and since their children were born they have moved between Canada and Northern Ireland several times. The first time they moved to Canada was in 1978 because they felt it would be better to bring up their children somewhere neutral.

Hassan has only experienced a few problems here: once in 1973 and, more recently, when some children threw water bombs at his house. He has many friends from here and his philosophy is to give trust and respect no matter what and to avoid bad feeling with others.

Although Hassan likes Northern Ireland, he feels Canada is his home and hopes to move back there eventually.

Achievements and Contributions

Hassan has worked in many different jobs over the years and has never been concerned with the status of any work. However, whatever his work, he has done well and been promoted. Since living in Kuwait, he has played in bands and has enjoyed some success:

"Even in Kuwait I was in a rock band, so when I got back to Jordan, I decided to start another band. It was the first local band ever and eventually it became well-known".

After moving to the UK, he joined a rock band in London which was offered a recording contract. Later, in Northern Ireland, he was with a Showband called 'Springfield' which played all over the Province.

He started his current post as a Community Development Worker with the Northern Ireland Muslim Family Association earlier this year. He sees his role as promoting the integration of the Muslim community whilst maintaining their identity. Hassan organises many activities and runs workshops on Islam and Muslim culture.

Last year, he organised a pilgrimage to Mecca for a hundred pilgrims and was very ill because of the work involved. He says that he paid for his pilgrimage with hardship.

Thoughts on the future

Hassan would like to see more for young people to do here. He feels the younger generation is the product of the 'Troubles' and this can make things difficult for them. Young people, he says, have so much energy, but limited ways in which to expend it. He believes that things are getting better here with more people travelling outside Northern Ireland. He also feels there is not a lot of racism but rather, recognition of difference.

Dr Farhat Manzoor

Dr Manzoor was born in Pakistan, but lived in Northern Ireland from the age of five. She now lives in Solihull, West Midlands and is, by profession, a Public Relations Officer.

Living in Northern Ireland

Although now living in England, Dr Manzoor's family still live in Northern Ireland and she visits them and friends on a regular basis.

Her experience of living in Northern Ireland has been a pleasant one. Although Dr Manzoor is aware that some people have experienced racism, she feels she has been very lucky in this respect, not having personally had any problems. Although, she says, during the 'Troubles' it was difficult here, she feels that "Northern Ireland did have less social crimes than the mainland" and can see the difference now that she lives in England. She has found that people in Northern Ireland are generally friendlier and more willing to help than elsewhere in the UK. Also, she believes that the education system in Northern Ireland is better with the standards in some schools seemingly higher than those in England. She wonders if this is related to Northern Ireland still having the 11+.

Achievements and Contributions

Dr Manzoor was educated in Northern Ireland and graduated from the University or Ulster with a BA (Hons) in Modern Studies. She then completed her PhD and her research concerned The Political History of Abortion in Northern Ireland.

She has recently completed research into Professional Values during the Troubles which was funded by The Nufflield Trust and this will be published this year (2005). The research was concerned with whether medical professionals in Northern Ireland were able to treat patients from the 'other community' in the same way as those from their own community.

She is currently applying for funding to research the migration pattern of doctors from South Asia into the UK from the 1960s onwards.

Dr Manzoor still attends functions held by the Muslim community in Northern Ireland and keeps some contact with the Belfast Islamic Centre.

Thoughts on the future

Dr Manzoor would like to see much more involvement by the Muslim community in Northern Irish society. She believes that they should become more involved in the decision making processes, including being more active politically. She feels that the Muslim community has much to offer Northern Ireland and through taking part in politics, they will be able to contribute their varied experiences and wide range of expertise, benefiting both the wider society and the Muslim community itself.

Mr Shuyb Miah

Shuyb is originally from Bangladesh and lives in Bangor, Co. Down. He came to the UK when he was nine and lived in Leeds for most of his life. He works as a Home/School Liaison Officer in the English as an Additional Language (EAL) Department of the South Eastern Education and Library Board (SEELB).

Living in Northern Ireland

Shuyb settled in Northern Ireland eight years ago, although he had been visiting regularly since 1987. He moved here because of family connections and was involved in the family business. He likes the lifestyle here, enjoys the sea and the countryside and finds the people "wonderful". He also found it very quiet, with a slower pace of life than in England. Shuyb's brother has been here since the middle of the 1980s and his uncle has been here even longer.

Prior to 9/11, Shuyb feels there were few problems for Muslims in Northern Ireland and had always found people here very friendly. Unfortunately, he believes that this has changed recently. It is, he feels, particularly difficult if someone works in the wider community rather than, for example, in a family run business. He talked about homes now being targeted and, indeed, his own home was attacked just a few months ago and graffiti put on the door saying 'Pakis Out'. This was very disturbing because it happened at night and made Shuyb feel quite vulnerable since his house had obviously been singled out. He is saddened by these changes because, before they occurred, he was comfortable going anywhere, but now he feels on edge and the need to be always on his guard. This type of victimisation is completely different from the more anonymous type of verbal abuse which occurred before – now it is personal. Since 9/11 the Mosque has also been targeted with the doors kicked in and windows broken. This, again, was frightening, especially because children were inside attending reading classes. However, on another level, Northern Ireland is becoming more multi-cultural, for instance, in Belfast there are now many more people from different cultures and ethnic backgrounds.

Achievements and Contributions

Shuyb left school with few qualifications and drifted about for a while. However, he decided to go back into full-time education and, through this, gained a diploma in Business Studies. He also volunteered as a Youth Worker with Bangladeshi young people. At that age he was not sure what he wanted to do, but, after completing his diploma, he was recruited as a Curriculum Parental Support Worker and stayed in this post for seven years. This work was mainly based in schools and involved also parental support and community work. He recently completed his HNC in Business Studies and is now aiming to complete a Master's Degree. Eventually, he would like to do the Post Graduate Certificate in Education, planning to then move into careers guidance or teaching in secondary education.

Shuyb started working in his current post by chance. He was considering whether or not to stay in the family business when a vacancy came up for a part-time Bangladeshi Liaison Officer. The post was similar to his previous work in England so he decided to apply and was successful. The initial contract was for three days a week over eighteen months, but last year he was made full-time. He sees his work as not only supporting children and their families at school but also the wider educational purpose of raising awareness and understanding of different cultures. This, he feels, also helps to prepare other children for life in a multi-cultural society. Finally, part of his work, as he sees it, is to be a role model for the children he is working with.

Coming to the UK at nine had significant disadvantages for Shuyb, in that he missed most of his primary education and just about made it into the mainstream of secondary school. The type of work he does is very close to his heart, because he is supporting children who are in similar circumstances to those he was in.

"It makes me aware of what I missed and I wonder sometimes how I went through school – I sometimes have flashbacks and think 'I used to sit there staring at the wall'."

Shuyb feels he has always tried to close the educational achievement gap through gaining qualifications and spoke of the difficulties there are in competing with those who have been brought up here, especially when English is a person's second language. He says:

"Goals in life are individual, mine is education."

He feels he can relate to the children he works with and finds the job very rewarding in a completely different way to the rewards of working within the family business, which would have been mainly financial.

Within the Muslim community, Shuyb is on the Management Group of the Mosque and is also involved in the Bangladeshi community. He believes there are three different sides to life: school/work, religion and home and all three have to balance.

Thoughts on the future

He hopes that in the future people will look beyond colour, look at individuals, look at the commonalities and how we share things. He believes that "the core morals across religions are very similar", but says that people are not aware of this and this makes them feel vulnerable. The way forward, for Shuyb, is through communication and openness from both communities.

Dr Mamoun Mobayed & Mrs Wafa Dalati Mobayed

Dr and Mrs Mobayed are from Syria. They have three sons: the oldest and youngest being born in Dublin and the middle son in Limerick. Dr Mobayed is a Psychiatrist and Mrs Mobayed is a Teacher and an Author, having published several books. The family live in Belfast.

Living in Northern Ireland

Dr and Mrs Mobayed initially moved to Leeds where Dr Mobayed was studying English. After a few months, they moved to Dublin where he was working and training at St Patrick's Hospital. They stayed in the Republic of Ireland for about nine years, living in Dublin and Limerick, before moving to Belfast in 1990 for Dr Mobayed to take up a post at the City Hospital.

Mrs Mobayed's first impression of Northern Ireland was of a very dynamic society where people were very helpful and warm. Dr Mobayed says that their experience in Northern Ireland has been positive and overall they are very pleased with their life here. They have achieved many things, most importantly on the family level, with their three sons being very happy and doing well. Their sons are comfortable with their multiple identities – they are Muslim of Syrian origin, born in the Republic of Ireland, spending their early lives there and then living in Northern Ireland for the past fifteen years. They speak Arabic, read the classics, support Liverpool in football and Pakistan in cricket.

Achievements and Contributions

Dr Mamoun Mobayed

Dr Mobayed undertook training and research in the Republic of Ireland, completing his MSc in Psychiatry at Trinity College, Dublin. One of his special interests in psychiatry is trauma and he has done voluntary work in the West Bank of Palestine training health professionals in how to help traumatised children. He has published six books and is currently working on a book on Children's Identity. All the books are currently in Arabic although there are plans for translations into other languages.

After a period in the City Hospital, Dr Mobayed moved to the Mater Hospital and here he started seeing people on a daily basis with conditions related to the 'Troubles'. He found that being from outside Northern Ireland could be an advantage, making communication with patients more relaxed. In addition, he is involved in establishing the only treatment centre in Ireland for offenders with learning disabilities at Muckamore Abbey Hospital. He is also an Honorary Lecturer at Queen's University, Belfast, where he teaches the History of Islamic Medicine.

Dr Mobayed has worked in the Muslim community for many years, individually and through his involvement in several different organisations. He was President of both the Belfast Islamic Centre (BIC) and of the Northern Ireland Interfaith Forum (NIIF), of which he was a founder member. This latter group established the Quiet Room at Belfast International Airport, for people of any or no faith who need a quiet place to reflect. Through the NIIF, he has also been involved in educational work and awareness training. An example of this is the booklet produced by NIIF, called Check Up, which informs health professionals about the needs of different faiths. They also produce the Multi-Faith Calendar, which gives the dates of feasts and ceremonies of different faiths.

He is now involved in the Northern Ireland Muslim Family Association (NIMFA). The aims of this association are active integration but, at the same time, preservation of the Muslim identity. This was reflected by a joint event with Belfast City Council, organised in 2004 which involved planting Cedar trees, which are very good for the environment, near Belfast Castle. The planting was symbolic, to show that Muslims literally have roots here. Another project entails the Blood Bank coming to NIMFA so members can then donate blood.

Dr Mobayed is the Muslim Chaplin at Queen's University, visits colleges and schools to give talks on Islam and Islamic Cultures (he would argue there is not only one culture) and has delivered a course on Islamic Cultures at Queen's

University. He also offers workshops on parenting skills and was involved in producing a booklet on how faith can help in the recovery from trauma.

Mrs Wafa Dalati Mobayed

Mrs Mobayed has a degree in Arabic Language and Literature from Damascus University. While her children were young, she was a full-time mother, although she did teach Muslim children Arabic and Qur'anic studies at Dunmurry Primary School. After the children started school she taught Arabic at Queen's University for seven years and also began to write. She has published five works with the sixth being launched shortly. The books are in Arabic but she hopes in the future they will be translated into English. Five of her books are fiction and one is a guide on 'How to become a writer'. This concept is unusual in Arabic culture because the ability to write is seen as a gift rather than a skill which can be learnt. She has also produced a collection of her own poetry, which will be considered for publication soon.

Her first story, The Old Stony One, is about an old building and is for teenagers. Her second book, The Scale, is a symbolic story of an innocent man who was a prisoner of conscience for fifteen years and it relates his dialogue about knowledge, justice and idealism after he left prison. A Crescent in the Snow of the Balkans, Mrs Mobayed's third novel, is about the Bosnian conflict and is anti-war. Her last novel, The One Who Lives Between Two Eras, addresses some of the current difficulties for Muslims. It is based in London and is about Muslim families who exist 'as if' between two eras or cultures. The novel being currently published is called The Page and is about the value of manuscripts and the need to take knowledge from these. It is told through the story of a writer who is trying to find a subject to write about which is beyond the forty two categories which are already known to exist. Mrs Mobayed used this novel to test the techniques in the guide she wrote and has been told that this work has shown real development. Finally, she is currently working on a new novel which has the provisional title Beyond the Shadow.

Ajwad

This name means 'the one who looks for the best'. Ajwad went to Dunmurry Primary School and then Methodist College. He is now in his final year of Medicine at Queen's and is interested in neurology, currently thinking about training in Psychiatry with a specialism in neurology. Ajwad is a keen cricketer and an avid reader, currently reading Naim Chomsky. He taught himself about computers and has built one.

Emran

Emran was the name of Mary's father in Islamic literature and means 'habitation, long life or civilisation'. He is in his second year of Medicine, also at Queen's. Emran introduced cricket into the family – maybe because he shares his first name with Imran Khan. He is considerate and passionate about what he believes in. After his 'A' levels, he took a 'gap year' and studied Arabic at Damascus University. This summer he attended a two week course in London on Islamic Knowledge.

Tamim

Tamim is doing his 'A' levels in Politics, Religious Education, English and Biology at Methodist College and reads a lot. He is passionate about African American history and Irish history. Tamim is also keen on Sociology, Psychology and Media and his work placement was with the BBC. When he was a child, he thought about producing a book called 'My City' containing photographs of Belfast because it is his city. Tamim has not decided yet what he wants to do in the future because his interests are so wide.

Thoughts on the future

Both Dr & Mrs Mobayed are optimistic that the 'Peace Process' will be successful. With this, Dr Mobayed hopes that the whole community will start to acknowledge the different cultures living here and reach the stage where they will celebrate diversity and join together for festivals and cultural events. He also hopes people will start to recognise that it is possible to have multiple identities and appreciate the richness of this.

Dr Mobayed believes the responsibility for good relations is a joint one. It is important for Muslims to reach out and communicate with the wider community. However, in order for Muslims to feel completely part of society and be accepted as such, the wider community must also initiate changes. These include schools being encouraged to cover all religions in Religious Education and offering Arabic at GCSE and 'A' level.

He feels the atrocities which happened in London, in July 2005, have confused the message that Muslims care about the welfare of this society. It is important, he believes, that Muslims work to try to dispel the myths and stereotypes about Muslims and Islam.

"Muslims should be like sugar in tea: it is diluted but keeps its flavour and sweetens the society".

Finally, Dr Mobayed hopes that women will increasingly take their natural role within the Muslim community to influence the future.

Dr. Suleyman S. Nalbant

Dr Nalbant is originally from Ankara, Turkey. He is married and they have four children, aged fifteen, thirteen, seven and one year. He and his family moved to Northern Ireland in January, 2001 and their youngest child was born here. The family live in Coleraine.

Living in Northern Ireland

Dr Nalbant came here to work in research. He is a Seismologist working with Professor John McCloskey and Dr. Sandy Steacy from the Geophysics Research Group, University of Ulster. He and his family moved to Coleraine when he joined the University of Ulster.

His experiences in Northern Ireland have all been positive. The family have never had any problems or experienced discrimination. Although having heard of the potential for sectarian clashes here, Dr Nalbant has never seen anything like that and feels the Peace Process is working well, especially in Coleraine. He has found people in the University to be helpful and friendly and this is one of the factors which encouraged the family to settle here. Originally they came for two years, but now have been here for almost five. The whole family like living here having made friends and settled well. The children, especially, are happy in their schools. Dr Nalbant says: "my wife is happy to be here, the children are happy to be here and they find the educational system is better than Turkey".

Achievements and Contributions

Dr. Nalbant's specialism is earthquake science. This is an important area of research for Turkey, because earthquakes are quite active there. Particularly since the 1999 Izmit earthquake, there has been much more research than before. He has been involved in modelling of stress perturbation due to earthquakes. The Geophysics Research Group in Coleraine was leading a European Community project consisting of UK, Italy, France, Czech Republic, Ireland and Greece. Experienced research institutions from each country gathered together on this project. There was a vacancy for another researcher, so Dr Nalbant applied and was successful. The work involved was parallel to that which he had been involved in for his PhD thesis and he had published a couple of papers on earthquakes before coming here.

The European Community Project was successfully completed in 2003 and since then, the work of the group has continued, focussing on modelling the effects of earthquakes. They modelled the December 2004 earthquake which occurred in Sumatra. This was possibly the second largest and deadliest earthquake which has occurred in the last century, killing almost 300,000 people. Through modelling its stress fields, they were able to identify two specific areas posing high seismic risk. They quickly published their findings and ten days later on 28th March, another earthquake occurred in one of the locations they had indicated in the paper.

The public view is, he says, that they predict earthquakes, although, technically they are not predicting because they cannot yet give precise timings of when one will occur. However, they are able to give the correct locations. With the techniques being used, the research team are also able to give the approximate magnitude. The paper attracted substantial media attention, both in the UK and internationally, particularly because of its accuracy concerning the second location. Because of this success, the University received a lot of attention which resulted in good publicity.

Dr Nalbant tries to be active in the Muslim community in Coleraine. It is quite a small community and each Friday at prayers there are around twenty-five or thirty people. The community tries to get together every one or two months, using one of the University halls. They also invite new students from Muslim countries to give them the opportunity to meet other Muslims. He has, in addition, been involved in establishing a Turkish Association. One of the main aims of this group is cross-cultural dialogue to encourage respect and tolerance between the different beliefs.

The Association is based in Belfast, where most of the Turkish community lives. Through its aims, it seeks to support couples and families where one partner is from Turkey and the other is from Northern Ireland. In particular, the group tries to support the children, who may be confused because of the two cultural influences. They are starting Turkish language classes every Saturday in the Multi-Cultural Resource Centre, which are being funded by 'Awards for All'. They also hope to arrange cultural activities for religious and national days so that children can become familiar with the language, culture and food of Turkey.

Thoughts on the future

Dr Nalbant would like there to be a Prayer Room in the University. The present room, which is shared with the Christian groups, is not large enough for Friday prayers because the numbers of people attending prayers is growing, as are the numbers of Muslim students. He feels the University has been very supportive and helpful so far and hopes that they will be able to facilitate the need for a Prayer Room.

Br. Javaid Naveed

Br. Javaid is a Businessman and originally from Pakistan. He is married with a three year old daughter and his wife, who is also of Pakistani origin, was brought up in Northern Ireland. The family live in Belfast.

Living in Northern Ireland

Br. Javaid came to Northern Ireland in 1984 when he was twenty-one, because of his marriage, which was arranged. He says that it was a totally different world to the one he was used to in terms of religion, culture and, especially, the weather. Although he arrived in August, it was cold and raining, which was the complete opposite to Pakistan.

When Br. Javaid came here, the 'Troubles' were still quite severe and the centre where his business was located was bombed twice. He had never experienced anything like this in Pakistan, especially since he came from one of the more remote cities. However, he says, "as time goes on you get used to the situation: checkpoints, bomb scares or explosions". Br. Javaid was aware of the situation in Northern Ireland before he came here, because he had always had an interest in world affairs. Consequently, he was a little apprehensive about coming, but once here, felt it was completely different to how it was portrayed in the media. The image abroad was that there was fighting everywhere, rather than it being concentrated in particular areas.

Br. Javaid feels he is fairly easy going and adaptable and that helped him when he moved here, although he admits to being lonely. He missed his family very much, particularly since he was the youngest in the family and had everything done for him as a child. However, the business kept him very busy and this also helped him to settle.

Living in Northern Ireland has generally been a good experience for Br. Javaid and, although he has experienced some incidences of name calling, says he likes living here. He has found people from both the Protestant and Catholic communities friendly and has made many friends from within the local communities.

Achievements and Contributions

Before coming to Northern Ireland, Br. Javaid had worked in a Bank for three years. A few months after he arrived, he and his wife opened their own shop in High Street, Belfast. They worked hard and gradually expanded their business into four shops, two ladies and children's fashion shops and two giftware shops. They still have two shops, although no longer in High Street and also a takeaway business. Br. Javaid says, when he came here he had nothing, but always had the aim to have his own business. Through hard work, he and his wife have built up and expanded their business to what it is now.

Since coming here, Br. Javaid has been involved in various organisations. He was active in the Belfast Islamic Centre for eight years as the Treasurer and was also a member of the Executive Committee of the Interfaith Forum. He was formerly the Chair and Vice-Chair of the Northern Ireland Council for Ethnic Minorities (NICEM) and is still a member of the Executive Committee. He is both the President of the Pakistani Cultural Association, the Vice-Chair of the Northern Ireland Muslim Families Association (NIMFA) and, in addition, the Chair of the Multi-National Sports Centre, which he and some others are in the process of setting up. Br. Javaid has also been a member of several advisory committees and currently sits on the Northern Ireland Race Forum, which is an inter-departmental forum with representatives from minority ethnic groups and the Multi-cultural Advisory Group for the PSNI. Through his work with NICEM, Br. Javaid met people from many different backgrounds. He remembers a meeting with Mo Mowlam, who has recently died, describing her as a very nice lady and very 'down to earth'.

He says he always felt it was important to help his Pakistani and Muslim brothers and personally offers support on welfare and social problems. He also offers support to people who have just arrived in Northern Ireland, for instance, through interpreting, giving 'cultural' advice on living here or practical information on, for example, where to buy halal meat.

Within the Pakistan Cultural Association, Br. Javaid organised the first Pakistani Independence Day celebration in around 2000 and this year is planning also an Eid show for the first time, involving both the Muslim and local community. Br. Javaid has always felt it was important to open up these events to both the local and other minority ethnic communities. He feels that this type of event does help different groups to integrate and break down barriers.

Through Br. Javaid's various businesses he contributes significantly to the Northern Ireland economy, both through taxes and employing people from the local community. He is also the representative in Northern Ireland of the Vice-Consular of Pakistan and helps people with visa and passport issues, as well as advising local business on, for example, export regulations. Before Br. Javaid took on this role, people had to travel to Glasgow.

Thoughts on the future

For the future, Br. Javaid plans to arrange classes in Urdu and Pakistani Culture for children within the Pakistani Cultural Association which, he believes, will help children feel more at home when they visit Pakistan. He hopes that both of the Northern Irish communities continue to move towards peace and would like the Muslim community to also be involved in this. Ultimately, he would like to see "everyone in Northern Ireland living together as a family, regardless of religion, culture or colour – a family of human beings, respecting each other".

Finally, he would like to appeal to the Muslim Community to unite because a united community is a strong community and can achieve so much more.

Dr Imad Omer

Dr Omer is originally from Sudan and is a Medical Doctor, specialising in gynaecology and obstetrics. He is married with three daughters (eight, six and three years) and one son who is a year old. His wife is also from Sudan and a Doctor, but is now a full-time mother. The family live in Lisburn.

Living in Northern Ireland

The wish to come to Northern Ireland originated with Dr Omer's aunt, who had studied for her PhD at Queen's University between 1976 and 1982. She used to talk about Belfast, particularly how nice people were here.

Dr Omer initially came to London and was looking for a job, but the idea of coming to Northern Ireland was still in his mind. He contacted a friend who was working in Enniskillen, who spoke to one of her Professors and, consequently, he was offered a job, starting his clinical attachment there in 1999. Since he had always wanted to visit Northern Ireland, Dr Omer was very excited about coming here. He was not 'put of' by the conflict because, as he says, "there are also problems in my country ... there are problems everywhere". He was, instead, curious, because what he had heard about the 'Troubles' in the media did not reflect what he had been told by his aunt.

Overall, Dr Omer feels his time in Northern Ireland has been very positive. He has achieved what he wanted to professionally and was not disappointed by the place. He has made many friends and has a good relationship with his neighbours and colleagues, finding them very kind and helpful. Where Dr Omer works, there are people from many different religions and he has found that relationships are very good between people from various backgrounds. He feels that people respond to each other as human beings first and foremost, not on the basis of religion. Although he misses friends and family from Sudan, he feels that his friends here are like his family now and considers Northern Ireland his home.

Achievements and Contributions

After leaving school at eighteen, Dr Omer studied Medicine in Egypt, staying there for over six years. He then worked in Sudan and completed his postgraduate degree, before going to Saudi Arabia to work. He undertook further training in Northern Ireland and during his clinical attachment, worked at several different hospitals. He joined the Mater Hospital in 2002 and, in August 2005, will be starting a new post at the Royal Maternity. During medical school he developed an interest in obstetrics and decided to specialise in this after graduating. He feels this area is different to others in medicine because the patients are not usually ill and are expecting something nice.

In terms of the Muslim community, Dr Omer's involvement is limited by the demands of his work and he cannot attend the Mosque very often, even for Friday prayer. However, he says that Muslims can pray anywhere so he just takes a few minutes wherever he is at the time. His daughters attend the classes in Arabic and Qur'anic Studies at Northern Ireland Muslim Family Association (NIMFA) every Friday evening and Sunday morning. He also tries to attend meetings and activities arranged by NIMFA.

Thoughts on the future

Dr Omer says that Islam, like other religions, stresses the importance of respect and having good relations with other people. He believes the events in London in July 2005, do not reflect the true meaning of Islam and that no true Muslim would accept these as being right. He hopes that people will understand this and also understand more about Islam and Muslims so they will recognise that Muslims are good and decent people. He also hopes for a closer relationship between the wider community and an increased awareness of the good things about Islam.

Professor Kader Parahoo

Professor Parahoo is originally from Mauritius, moving to England in 1973 to study and then Northern Ireland in 1986 take up a post of Lecturer at the University of Ulster. By profession, he is an Academic and he is married with three children – two girls who are nine and eight years old and a boy of six. His wife is from Northern Ireland and the family live in Portstewart.

Living in Northern Ireland

The decision to come to Northern Ireland was based on a previous holiday in Ireland. Professor Parahoo thought the country was beautiful and found the people very friendly. Consequently, when a job was advertised for a Lecturer in Nursing at the University of Ulster he applied for it and was selected. He was offered similar jobs in England but turned them down because when he came over here and met people, he felt that Northern Ireland was where he would like to settle.

Professor Parahoo says that he has had very positive experiences here, finding Northern Irish people very friendly, respectful and helpful. One of the first things he noticed was how helpful people were when asked for directions:

"It is surprising how people go out of their way and walk a long way to show you where something is. You won't find this in many other places".

He finds Northern Ireland similar in many ways to Mauritius:

"In many ways, perhaps what attracts me here is that the community life and the way the people are is very similar to ... Mauritius. Over there as well, people are very helpful, very friendly and they value family life. They respect elders and so on and church going is the same and that is probably what subconsciously attracts me here because I find a lot of similarities between us."

Although Professor Parahoo has had very good offers of work from elsewhere, he has turned them down at the last minute when he realised what Northern Ireland meant to him. He has decided that Northern Ireland is where he wants to spend the rest of his life.

Achievements and Contributions

As mentioned earlier, Professor Parahoo's first post at the University of Ulster was as a Lecturer in Nursing, but after five years he was promoted to Senior Lecturer. Recently, he was promoted to Professor in Nursing and Health Research and, earlier this year, he was appointed the Director for the Institute of Nursing Research. He is very happy at the University of Ulster, finding it a good place to work.

Professor Parahoo is a member of various committees in the NHS Trusts and the Department of Health. He is also involved in cross-border projects with other researchers in the South of Ireland. His speciality is nursing research; developing research and practice and also teaching in this area. Through his research role he is closely in touch with practitioners and managers in the Health Service. His work contributes to the development of a better Health Service, through the education and training of practitioners. Many of his students go on to take up important posts within the Health Service.

In 1997 he wrote a book Nursing Research: Principles, Process and Issues, (published by Palgrave), which is a best seller in the UK. This book has contributed significantly to health professionals' understanding of what research is and the second edition will be published shortly.

Within his professional role, Professor Parahoo contributes significantly to Northern Irish society through his focus on the improvement of health care practice in the Province. Together with his family, he takes an active part in community life in Portstewart and he is also involved in the Muslim community in Coleraine and the 'triangle' area.

Thoughts on the future

Professor Parahoo would like to see more local facilities for Muslims such as a Mosque and places to buy halal food. However, he feels that currently there are probably not enough Muslims in the area for these things to happen.

Mrs Nazneen Raza

Mrs Raza was born and brought up in India and then moved to Pakistan after High School. She married after completing her MA and came to Northern Ireland in 1979 to join her husband, Dr Syed H Raza. They live in South Belfast and have four sons. Their eldest son graduated with a degree in Accountancy and currently lives and works in London; their second son completed a degree in Arts and Design and their third son is studying for a degree in Drama at Kingston University. Their youngest son is still at home and is doing his GCSE's this year.

Living in Northern Ireland

Mrs Raza says that Northern Ireland was a completely different world to the one she was used to – "it was East and this is West". The weather, in particular, was difficult to get used to, however, she found people here were very helpful and nice. Not being able to see her family because they were far away, missing

139

the social life she had in Karachi and the language barrier, left Mrs Raza feeling very isolated. Even though she had some friends, she still spent a lot of time on her own and she suffered from depression for a year. Through keeping busy with the children and house and talking with friends, Mrs Raza eventually started to settle down and feel better, but it was very difficult at first.

Bringing up children here can, says Mrs Raza, be difficult because they are surrounded by a different culture. She focused on teaching her children about her culture and Islam. Her boys were all born and educated here and while at school they all studied Religious Education. She felt this was good, because then she would discuss with them what Islam says. She says: "Children always want to compare and see what the differences are". She feels it was more difficult to pass on culture because here is very different.

Al-Nisa is, says Mrs Raza, a very important support for Muslim women in Northern Ireland; helping to overcome isolation, giving support with problems and organising educational classes. She feels if Al-Nisa had been in existence when she came, things would not have been so difficult for her.

Achievements and Contributions

After graduating with a BA in Islamic Studies, Mrs Raza then completed an MA in the same subject. When she came to Northern Ireland she studied English because, although she had learnt it as a child in Pakistan, it was very different having to use it on a daily basis. She also attended meetings organised by the British Council for overseas wives. While her children were young, Mrs Raza was too busy to become very involved in community activities, so she only really attended the Mosque. However, once they were a little older, she started to help with teaching children to read the Qur'an at the Belfast Islamic Centre (BIC). Later some girls said they wanted to learn Urdu, so she started to teach this as well and did this for three or four years. She became involved in the informal Women's Group at BIC, almost from its beginning. Her involvement continued through the development from the informal group to the formal Women's Group (BIC) and finally into the setting up of Al-Nisa as an independent organisation. She was, then, one of the founder members of Al-Nisa and has been volunteering for them in various roles ever since. Within Al-Nisa, Mrs Raza continued with her teaching, offering classes in Qur'anic Teachings for adults. She also still teaches some children Islamic Studies. Her work in Al-Nisa also includes administration and supervising the premises.

Mrs Raza believes it is important to help other people. She says that this was how she was brought up and something which is central to Islam. As an individual she has helped people by keeping them company, looking after their children and cooking for people who are sick. She does not restrict herself to helping members of the Muslim community but, rather, anyone who needs help.

In terms of the wider community, Mrs Raza has also volunteered for other organisations such as fundraising for the Salvation Army and the Northern Ireland Association for the Blind, collecting door to door and raising funds when there are emergencies in other countries. She says this is something she and other members of Al-Nisa are pleased to do.

Hopes for the Future

Mrs Raza feels that Muslims here are doing very well financially and most are professionals or business people. It is, she says, a challenge for people to move to a different country and, as a result, they then work very hard. She hopes that the Muslim community will continue to work together to benefit Northern Ireland. She believes this is important because Islam also teaches that Muslims must work to benefit all humanity, not just Muslims. She further hopes that the Muslim community will work together for the benefit of its members and the wider community. She thinks that, with the establishment of Al-Nisa by Mrs Khan, Muslim women should take full advantage of it, by participating in its activities, within the framework of Islamic faith and culture. They should also make every effort to develop good relationships with the wider community. She hopes that the younger generation will also make every effort to get involved with the activities of Al-Nisa, which will ensure its existence and make it a more dynamic organisation for all age groups.

Dr Syed Hassan Raza

Dr Raza attended primary school in Dehli, India. After partition, his family moved to Lahore in Pakistan. Dr Raza married Nazneen in 1979 and they have four sons. (see separate entry for Mrs Nazneen Raza and Vali Raza)

Living in Northern Ireland

Dr Raza came to Northern Ireland to study. His parents wanted him to get married, but he felt he needed to complete his studies first. He was the first in his family to go abroad.

Dr Raza stayed a week in London before coming to Belfast. On his flight to Belfast, he met an Indian Doctor who helped him to find his way to his accommodation. Dr Raza says that he cried when the Doctor left. He arrived in Belfast on a Sunday and everything was closed. This was a major contrast to Lahore and London, so his first impression was quite depressing. He asked his landlady if there were any other people from India or Pakistan and she directed him to the British Council.

Achievements and Contributions

Dr Raza's first degree was in Physics and after graduating he then completed his MSc. Between 1960 and 1965, he worked as a Lecturer in Physics at

Foreman Christian College, Lahore. This was one of the best Colleges in Pakistan, with a very high status and was run by the American Presbyterian Church. Dr Raza applied to do an MSc in Electronics in the UK, but the College didn't want him to leave. However, he felt it was important to continue with his studies. He received three offers from universities in the UK and chose Queen's University, Belfast.

In 1967, Dr Raza completed his MSc in Electronics and was offered a post to complete his PhD. His research area was silicon technology and Queen's was one of three pioneering universities in this research area in the UK, the others being Southampton and Edinburgh. He completed his PhD in 1972 and although he was offered a Grade 20 post in Pakistan, decided to stay in Belfast. He did consider moving to Silicon Valley in the US, but decided not to because of the disruption to the family.

He started work as a Research Officer, later being promoted to Senior Research Officer and when he retired in 2003 he had reached the position of Senior Research Fellow in the Electrical and Electronic Engineering Department. His speciality was developments in silicon technology and fabrication of Semi-conductor Integrated Circuits. He started working with 2" diameter silicon wafers which were the start of smaller integrated circuits. He says of his work "it was my hobby, my work, my entertainment, I loved my work". Dr Raza often worked seven days a week and made many personal sacrifices to pursue his research.

Dr Raza has published in numerous academic journals and through the contractual work undertaken by Queen's, has developed several patents in the Information Technology field. Particularly, he has worked on semi-conductor technology; developing bonding techniques to produce NP bonded silicon wafers. Either side can then be 'grinded' down and polished to 1/100th of a millimetre, or less, for fabrication of high density high speed integrated circuits. The bonding process bonds without wires and means the materials are kept pure.

Because of the dedication to his work Dr Raza had little time for community involvement and his major contribution to Northern Ireland has been through the research and contractual work he undertook for industry and educational institutions during his time at Queen's.

Thoughts on the future

Dr Raza's hopes for the future relationship between the Muslim community and the indigenous population in Northern Ireland is that they will live in

143

harmony, understanding and respecting one another's cultural, social and religious values and traditions. He believes that the Muslim community will help to shape the future generations to contribute towards the well being of all who inhabitant this island, drawing on the best traditions and in the most effective way possible. He finishes with the statement: "God willing".

Mr Vali Raza

Vali is nineteen years old and has passed his 11+, his GCSE's and 'A' levels in Politics, Maths and Drama, for which he achieved an honour grade. He was also a prefect. In 2000 he came third in the Belfast Festival Drama Competition. He has taken part in plays at school and had a part in 'School for Scandal'. He has also had parts as an extra in movies. Until recently, he was working for Clarkes Shoes as a Stockroom Manager. He started there in October, 2004 and was promoted in March, 2005. He has now moved to London to study a BA (Hons) in Acting, Theatre and Media at Kingston College.

The computer system in Al-Nisa was set up by Vali and he also maintains it, as well as helping with any heavy work which needs doing. He plays right wing in hockey and enjoys rowing, squash and football. Vali is a member of the Muslim Youth Group and a Youth Group at Fisherwick Church. He also volunteers with a junior youth group helping to organise activities for 7 – 8 year olds.

Vali feels living as a Muslim in Northern Ireland has been "OK" and has found most people here to be open minded.

Mr Ahmed and Mrs (Dr) Fouzia Sharieff

Mr Sharieff is originally from India, and is a Chemical Engineer by profession. He married in 1975 and his wife, Dr Fouzia Sharieff, is a Psychiatrist who is also originally from India. They have two children, born in 1976 and 1977 who were born, brought up and educated in Northern Ireland. Both children went to university in London to train as medical doctors. Their daughter, who is a GP, is married to a Hospital Doctor and now lives in London. Their son works in Accident and Emergency in Coleraine Area Hospital. Mr and Dr Sharieff moved to the Coleraine area on Mr Sharieff's retirement.

Living in Northern Ireland

Mr Sharieff came to Northern Ireland because he had been offered a post here and his wife, Dr Sharieff, joined him when they got married. He initially planned to come to the UK for a few years to study and work before returning to India, however, he decided to stay. He says:

"Ireland is wonderful, the schools are good and have discipline and the quality of life is very high. You bump into people you know all the time and strangers say 'good morning'. Neighbours look out for each other and there is a real sense of community".

Their children were looked after by a Mrs McLaughlin, who was a local woman and were influenced by this, says Mr Sharieff: "they are Irish and, although they went to England, Northern Ireland is still their home, especially Eglinton Village in Co Londonderry, where they grew up".

There were some difficulties, living as a Muslim in the 1970s. For instance, it was difficult to find halal meat and Indian spices. However, they managed to buy their meat directly from the abattoir and there is a longstanding shop in Omagh where they were able to buy spices. Now, however, everything is much easily available. Another difficulty was, until recently, food labels did not necessarily list all ingredients. Consequently, Muslims could inadvertently buy something which contained ingredients which were forbidden to eat but, again, things are much easier now because labels are more comprehensive.

Mr Sharieff describes himself and his family as follows: "We are British Muslims of Indian origin and living in Northern Ireland".

Achievements and Contributions

Mr Ahmed Sharieff

Mr Sharieff qualified as a Chemical Engineer in India and came to the UK in 1965. He worked in Manchester with a chemical manufacturer for six years then went to Birmingham to do a postgraduate qualification. After he finished his postgraduate studies in 1973, the Dupont Company in Northern Ireland offered him a job and he worked there until he retired.

Mr Sharieff took early retirement in 1993 and decided to move to Coleraine. In retirement, Mr Sharieff is an active volunteer, donating his time and his experience. He says: "The community has been good to us and now is the time to put something back". He volunteers with UNICEF, promoting the organisation and fundraising and also for Age Concern as an advocate. In the latter role, he supports the elderly with issues such as health, finance, filling in forms and hospital visits. He is a member of the local Probus Club and the Men's Fellowship and also enjoys golf. For Mr and Dr Sharieff it is important that they try to participate in all aspects of the community.

Mrs (Dr) Fouzia Sharieff

Dr Sharieff trained as a Psychiatrist and has been practicing since 1975. Currently she works as a locum, which means she can choose where she works and is able to take time off to do other things. She specialises in general psychiatry, depression, alcohol related problems and those who have been sexually abused. She has also treated people suffering from Post Traumatic Stress Disorder as a result of the Omagh bombing. Dr Sharieff came here in 1975, after her marriage. She was not sure what to expect when she came to Northern Ireland, especially because of the 'Troubles'. Shortly after she arrived she had a few very frightening experiences, for instance, a bomb scare in Littlewoods and, when she was pregnant, being near bombs in Foyle Street and not being able to get to her car. She recognises, however, that there was a day-to-day normality, even during the 'Troubles'. Although working, Dr Sharieff also volunteers with UNICEF. She also enjoys gardening and their garden has been opened for the National Trust in previous years. They both try to support international students by inviting them to their home and involving them in things which are happening and enjoy entertaining friends.

Thoughts on the future

The sense is that Mr and Dr Sharieff are happy with how their lives have gone so far in Northern Ireland and hope that the friendliness and helpfulness which first impressed them will continue. The main difficulty they see for the Muslim community in the Coleraine area is that it has no specific centre. However, they say the University of Ulster has been particularly helpful in allocating space for Friday prayers.

Mr Rafay Tariq

Rafay is of Pakistani descent and was born in Kuwait. He has just graduated with a degree in Actuarial and Financial Studies and currently lives in the family home at Warrenpoint.

Living in Northern Ireland

The Gulf War resulted in Rafay and his family having to leave Kuwait and they moved to Northern Ireland because his father was offered work here through his business contacts. His experience of living in Northern Ireland has been generally very positive and he says that he and his family have been well accepted by the local community in Warrenpoint. He has found discrimination to be negligible and believes that his quality of life in Northern Ireland has been much better than it would have been had the family remained in Kuwait.

Although Rafay attends Muslim community events from time to time and has friends within the Muslim community, most of his involvement is within the Northern Irish community. The majority of his friends are either Northern Irish or Irish and he would spend more time in this environment. Rafay would describe himself as: "liberal and secular in his viewpoints".

He feels that the Muslim community has generally integrated well into Northern Irish society and that Muslims have made significant and important contributions to the wider community.

Achievements and Contributions

Rafay achieved a First Class Honours Degree from University College, Dublin and plans to start working in London in the near future.

Thoughts on the future

Whilst Rafay believes the Muslim community has integrated well into Northern Irish society and makes an important contribution, he finds some members of the community 'old-fashioned'. He would like greater open-mindedness to allow further integration. An example he gives is that he would like to see Muslims represented in a wider range of professions: "rather than the usual few like medicine, engineering and law". However, he is hopeful that this type of integration will occur with the second and third generation of Muslims here.

He also hopes that:

"Muslims will continue to be well treated by the wider Northern Irish community, and will not suffer a backlash because of the recent or future actions of a tiny number of supposed Muslims that are involved in extremist activities in other parts of the world".

Dr Asghar A Wain & Dr Fakhra Butt

Dr Wain and Dr Butt are originally from Pakistan and are married with three children, two boys and a girl. Of the children, the eldest one was born in Karachi, the second was born in Gachsaran in Iran and the youngest was born in Scotland. They are both Medical Doctors and the family live in Lisburn.

Dr Wain

Living in Northern Ireland

The family came to Northern Ireland as a matter of chance. Dr Wain was working in Scotland until 1999 and had applied for a job here. At that time the situation was quite serious so they were very apprehensive about the move. When he came, he found it very difficult to understand the division between Protestants and Catholics.

He initially worked in a locum post for three months. His wife and children, at that time, had gone back to Pakistan because his wife needed to work for a year to complete Part II of her exam. Whilst here, Dr Wain was offered a permanent post in Down & Lisburn Trust. The friendliness of people here encouraged him to accept it and the rest of the family came to join him.

Dr Wain feels that long term settlement is dependent on two things, the community at large and the job opportunities. If these two aspects are

149

satisfactory, a person is likely to wish to stay. In particular, his children are attached to Northern Ireland and would not wish to move to another area.

Socialising, he says, can be difficult because here people tend to go to pubs. However, the family socialise at home or visit other people in their homes or picnic places. Dr Wain feels that generally people are inquisitive about Muslim culture in terms of their beliefs about alcohol, dress codes, prohibition of freely mixed gatherings (in terms of gender) and restrictions on intake of non-halal food.

The family have never experienced any difficulties as Muslims in Northern Ireland and have found people very friendly and understanding. Dr Wain believes that at work it is considered important to be a good human being, but says: "good clinical practice earns you respect".

Achievements and Contributions

Dr Wain graduated with an MBBS (Bachelor of Medicine and Surgery) in 1984 from Allama Iqbal Medical College in Lahore, Pakistan. He worked there for a year and then moved to Iran, working for about six years as a GP. In 1992, he came to Dublin and in 1995 completed his postgraduate exam FRCS (Fellow of the Royal College of Surgeons) in General Surgery. He was offered a post in Scotland and worked there for three years before moving to Northern Ireland. Initially, he worked in Lisburn and later Downpatrick Hospitals. He still works for Down & Lisburn Trust.

Dr Wain gains satisfaction from his work because it is concerned with helping people who are in trouble, who are not well. He sees it a very noble profession; one where a person can make a reasonable living and get satisfaction in what they do. He also feels that if someone is doing their job properly, people give them respect, especially in a small place. Although he thinks things have changed over the years, he feels the medical profession is still very well respected.

Thoughts on the future

Dr Wain wishes that people would stop describing terrorists as 'fundamentalist'. Terrorists are terrorists, full stop. For him "a fundamentalist Muslim is the best person on earth", someone who practices their religion in the best possible way and in its true spirit. He says: "for practising Muslims, to kill one person is like killing the whole of humanity but this is not how the media portray us".

He hopes that his children will progress and prosper and become good citizens and also, importantly, good human beings, accepting what is positive in society and working to improve it. He also hopes for a system where it does not matter what ethnic origin someone has; that anyone who deserves it, shall rise to the top.

He believes that there is a need for a broad based Religious Education in schools, that children should be taught different religions so that people become aware of the various beliefs. Best practices in different religions should also be emphasised. He would not want separate schools for different religions because, he feels, this would cause divisions. Rather, he would like a religious education, which is common to all and where everyone's religion is respected.

Dr Butt

Achievements and Contributions

Dr Butt graduated as MBBS (Bachelor of Medicine and Surgery) from Nawab Shah Medical College, Pakistan. She completed Part II of her postgraduate qualification MRCOG in Gynaecology and Obstetrics, in 2004, but has not yet worked in Northern Ireland.

As a full-time housewife and mother, Dr Butt has not had the same opportunities as her husband to meet "natives" of Northern Ireland, but she does meet other parents when she goes to pick up or drop off her daughter from school or when she goes shopping. She has never had any problems or experienced racism and is very comfortable here. She finished her studies last year and is now looking for work, but feels it will be very different from Pakistan, especially because the working day is longer in Northern Ireland; however this is balanced by only working for five days a week here.

Dr Butt says she likes Northern Ireland very much, finding people very friendly and the weather more comfortable than Scotland.

Thoughts on the future

Dr Butt would like Equality of Opportunity for everyone and feels there should be no discrimination or racism, because everyone is a human being.

Harris

Harris is sixteen years old and attends Friends School in Lisburn, having been there for four years. He is now in fifth year and has just finished his GCSE's including Additional Maths, three Sciences and Geography and is waiting for the results. He sat Maths GCSE in November 2004 and got an A*. Harris dropped

Religious Education (RE) in third year because it only covered Christianity. Instead, he used the resources in the school library to increase his knowledge of Islam. He now wonders if he should have taken RE to learn more about Christianity since, he says, the majority of people he knows are Christian. Harris feels "You can't just go through life just on what you know about your own religion". He plans to study Medicine in the future.

An enthusiastic sportsman, Harris plays cricket and hockey at school, as well as football with his friends and is a member of Lisburn Cricket Club. His religious beliefs play a big part in his life. Growing up as a Muslim here has not been particularly difficult, although he says racism and discrimination happen from time to time. He also thinks that most difficulties are not so much related to being Muslim but from being devout, believing practicing Christians may also face problems. Harris has spent most of his life here and sees himself as more a British person than Pakistani, although he was born there. He feels he has managed to integrate here without sacrificing his own beliefs.

Usama

Usama is thirteen years old and was born in Iran, but then moved to Pakistan after a few months, later moving to Scotland and then Northern Ireland. He is in his second year, also at Friends, and has just finished his summer exams, believing they went quite well. Biology is his favourite subject and he is also interested in Information Technology. He plays cricket for Ulster and was a member of the team, which played in the 'Inter-Pros' this year in Dublin. In this competition teams from the four Provinces play against each other and the Ulster team came second. He also plays hockey for South Antrim.

He feels it is "OK" being a Muslim in Northern Ireland, finding most people friendly, although acknowledging not everyone is. Moving so much has meant making friends is sometimes difficult, however, he says he has used to moving. He has now lived in Northern Ireland for four years but is not sure if they will stay here, however, he hopes the family will not move too often.

Hafsa

Hafsa is nine years old and was born in Scotland. She goes to Pond Park Primary School. She likes Art and is good at spelling and reading. She also likes hockey and enjoys playing with her friends, especially going to the park, which has swings, a roundabout and a slide.

Her teacher says she is a very good helper and that she likes to be involved in things. Hafsa makes tea for her father and presents it nicely with a napkin and dry fruit and has helped her mum to make jelly for a party. She also dusts at the weekend.

Hafsa's good friend has just moved to Canada and this has made her sad, however, Hafsa went to the airport with her friend to say goodbye. She hopes her friend will visit during the holidays.

Drs Jaweed and Farzana Wali

Both originally from India, Drs Jaweed and Farzana Wali have lived in Northern Ireland since 1981. They have a son and daughter, both of whom were educated here but are now living in London. They moved to Coleraine in 1986.

Living in Northern Ireland

Drs Jaweed and Farzana Wali say coming to Northern Ireland was an accident. Prior to coming to here they had worked in Iran and the US. They came to Northern Ireland to do their Plab test and Dr Jaweed Wali was offered a job immediately in Omagh. When they moved here, the 'Troubles' were quite severe, however, they were immediately impressed by the friendliness of the people here and how welcoming they were. As a Surgeon in Derry, Dr Jaweed Wali has treated bomb victims as well as people who have suffered punishment shootings, etc. but their personal experience has been good. They have not experienced racial discrimination either in their personal or professional lives, but feel that discrimination may be less likely for professional people.

The first three or four years were difficult in terms of access to appropriate food, but it is now much easier. A shop in Omagh has stocked Indian spices and food for many years.

Achievements and Contributions

Dr Jaweed Wali has been a Surgeon in the Causeway Hospital since 1986 and has also worked in Enniskillen, Lisburn and Derry. He is involved in teaching children about Islam, the principals of the faith and Arabic. As well as this, he has also taught the children comparative religions – Christianity, Hinduism and Judaism, emphasising the importance of interacting with people of other religions and respect for other beliefs. He is proud that all the students he has taught have become moderate adults who would have friends from all cultures and beliefs. Dr Jaweed Wali conducts Friday prayers and supports the local Muslim community by acting as an Iman. He believes that you need to give young people a strong foundation because, it is they who are the foundation of society.

Dr Jaweed Wali was previously a member of the Home Accident Prevention Committee. He is also a member of the Rotary Club and participates in their charitable works. He believes he may be the only Muslim member.

Although a qualified Medical Doctor, Dr Farzana Wali is now a housewife. She has spent most of her time in Northern Ireland bringing up her family but has also worked as a volunteer for the past twelve years for Oxfam.

Thoughts on the future

The Drs Wali, along with other Muslims in 'the triangle', are hoping to establish a place of worship for the Muslim community in the north of the Province.

Mr Mohammad Yasin

Mr Yasin was born and brought up in India until, in 1947, the part he lived in became Pakistan. He is married with four children and his wife was a Teacher in Pakistan. Three of his children still live in Northern Ireland and one is in England. He also has a grandchild. The family have lived in East Belfast since 1976.

He has always been interested in politics and was Secretary of the Students' Union at college, was a member of the first democratically elected government of Pakistan and was also a Shop Steward while working in Birmingham.

Living in Northern Ireland

Mr Yasin first came to Northern Ireland in 1960 to stay with his uncle and was planning to go to university. He had been influenced in moving here by magazines which said how wonderful the West was. His uncle had been in Northern Ireland since the 1930's and had a business manufacturing women's clothing, employing about thirteen girls.

When he arrived, Mr Yasin applied to Queen's University and was offered a place on the condition that he first studied English, so he enrolled in Shaftesbury Tutorial College and stayed there about three months. However, his uncle decided that Mr Yasin should become involved in the business so he had to postpone his education. He stayed in Belfast for about a year but was not really interested in the business so decided to return to Pakistan. After about six months some of his friends decided they would like to go to Northern Ireland, so they and Mr Yasin took a bus to London which cost 1,000 Rupees and took four weeks. This time Mr Yasin stayed for about fifteen months before returning to Pakistan. He became involved in politics and was elected as a member of the first democratic government in Pakistan. Disillusioned by the corruption, after two years he again left for the UK, this time for Birmingham, where he worked in a foundry for nearly three years.

In 1968 he again returned to Pakistan and, this time, decided to drive. He left the UK in December and because of bad weather, the journey took almost six weeks. Whilst in Pakistan he got married and, although he was then content to settle there, his wife wanted to move to the UK. Again, he moved to Birmingham where three of his children were born, remaining there until about 1974, when his uncle asked him to return to Belfast to work in the business. However, the business was in trouble and soon closed so Mr Yasin started to sell women's clothes in the markets and also travelled around much of Northern Ireland selling from a van.

Mr Yasin feels that there was a good relationship between people from Pakistan and local people because: "they were serving ordinary people and this meant that ordinary people were happy". He always found Irish people very genuine and has good friends from both sides of the community. In the late 1960's people from Pakistan were called 'black' but he feels that this was not meant to be insulting but rather was a way of identifying people. This was, he feels, unlike England where this term was used to be offensive.

Although he has heard of recent racist attacks he does not feel that discrimination is at the same level as in Britain. He believes that racial incidents are linked to economic factors and usually occur in deprived areas; he also believes that such incidents are exploited by the politicians.

Achievements and Contributions

Mr Yasin says that people from Pakistan changed the fashion and clothing business and the concept of markets in Northern Ireland. They were selling high fashion clothes for women at low prices, making the markets more competitive than shops and changing the type of customer who used them. At that time the clothing and fashion industry was dominated by people from Pakistan and India: the fabric suppliers were people from this region and so were the manufacturers and wholesalers. He believes that people from Pakistan were successful because they worked so hard and often the whole family was involved in the business. Women also worked and were considered equal partners.

Mr Yasin has never had ambitions for great wealth, his main concern was for his children to be well educated and, since all his children have achieved Masters Degrees, he feels he has achieved that.

Thoughts on the future

His hope for the future is that the good relationship between the Pakistani and the local communities continues. He is optimistic that this will happen because people from the Pakistani community are not competing with local people for work, they are either business people or professionals in, for example, the health service. In this sense, the Pakistani community is obviously contributing much to this society. He believes that, unless trouble is stirred up by politicians, the good relationship will continue. He feels particularly that the younger generation are no longer perceived as immigrants but are seen as being from here.

Mr Muhammad Yousaf
BSc, MBBS, FCPS, FRCS (I), FRCS (UGI/HPB), MPhil

Mr Yousaf is originally from Pakistan and a Surgeon by profession. He came to the UK to in 1996 and worked in England for sometime before moving to Northern Ireland in 1998. He is married with three children and lives with his family in Belfast.

Living in Northern Ireland

Mr Yousaf initially moved to Northern Ireland to continue with his training. However, he decided to settle here because he found the people were very friendly and the standard of the education for children was very high.

Of living in Northern Ireland, he says:

"I have been living as an honourable Muslim in Northern Ireland. People in my neighbourhood and workplace have been very supportive, understanding, co-operative and helpful. I never had any trouble leading a Muslim life here. My youngest son was born in Belfast, which further strengthened my bond with this part of the world. My children, especially, would never think of leaving Belfast".

Achievements and Contributions

Mr Yousaf was initially trained in Pakistan and has a Fellowship in Surgery from the College of Physicians and Surgeons of Pakistan (FCPS). In Northern Ireland, he worked for two years in General Surgery at Tyrone County Hospital, Omagh Hospital and Altnagelvin Hospital in Londonderry. He became a Specialist Registrar in general surgery in Northern Ireland's Higher Surgical Training programme in August 2000.

Over the last five years here, Mr Yousaf has worked as a trainee Surgeon. During this time, he completed his post graduation examinations including FRCS, FRCS (Gen) and MPhil. He is in his final years of training before being appointed as a Consultant. He has just completed a fellowship in pancreatic and liver surgery in Manchester. Mr. Yousaf specialises in surgery of cancers of the upper gastrointestinal tract, pancreas and liver. He is also an expert in laparoscopic surgery and in treating patients with complicated gallstone disease.

Mr Yousaf is very dedicated to his profession and in sincerely serving the people of Northern Ireland.

He has been actively participating in the Belfast Islamic Centre activities. Also, he has worked very hard to upgrade and improve the standard of Islamic education for Northern Ireland's Muslim children.

Thoughts on the future

Although there have been a few racial incidents in the past few months, Mr Yousaf feels the majority of people here are very broad minded and friendly. He believes that, with time, there will be better relations between the different communities in Northern Ireland.

Miss Zahbia Yousuf

Miss Yousuf was born and brought up in Northern Ireland and her parents are originally from India. She is a PhD student, currently living in London.

Living in Northern Ireland

Having grown up in Northern Ireland, Miss Yousuf sees herself as Northern Irish, but also as Muslim and Indian. She feels, in many ways, she had the best of both worlds, having friends from both the local community and the Muslim community. People in Northern Ireland were, she found, very tolerant towards the Muslim community and were interested to learn about both the Indian culture and the differences in beliefs between Islam and Christianity. At times she felt that the questions she was asked were "a little ignorant", but later realised that this was because there was very little awareness of other cultures here and people were "simply interested and attempting to understand ... more".

During the 1980's and 1990's, Miss Yousuf believes that there was limited awareness about the Muslim community in Northern Ireland. However, over the last ten years and particularly since the Good Friday Agreement, she feels that: "There has been a greater awareness of minorities in Northern Ireland ... There seem to be incentives ... to bridge the gap that existed, and the creation of cross-community programmes".

The Muslim community, she says:

"was very close knit and it felt very comforting to be part of something like that, because ... we were different in a way and it was good to be able to share that with similar people and also to feel free to do that whilst still being Northern Irish".

Living in London has made Miss Yousuf appreciate that Northern Ireland was "a great place ... to be a Muslim – people were tolerant and interested to know about Islam". She feels that because the Muslim community was such a small minority in Northern Ireland, "there was an acceptance of us that the mainland does not always have". The experience of living as a Muslim in Northern Ireland has, she believes, influenced her academic career and, especially, her choice of subject for her PhD, which focuses on peace processes and looks at Northern Ireland, Kashmir and Israel/Palestine.

Achievements and Contributions

Miss Yousuf has been very successful academically, gaining eleven GCSE's with eight at grade A* and three at grade A. She achieved the highest marks in Chemistry in Northern Ireland and the overall highest grades in the school. She also passed three 'A' levels at grade A before studying LLB Law Honours at University College, London where she was awarded a 2:1 degree. After finishing her degree Miss Yousuf completed an MA in International Peace and Security at King's College, London with the highest marks in her year and was accepted onto a PhD programme at the Department of War Studies at Kings's College, winning a scholarship from the Economic Social Research Council.

She has also been doing research with the Open University, involving ethnic minorities, the media and security which involved interviewing Muslim families within Northern Ireland.

Through her parents, Miss Yousuf maintains links with the Muslim community in Northern Ireland and participates in celebrations and events whenever possible. She remains in close contact with friends from Northern Ireland, many of whom now have moved to London, and she has organised school reunions both there and in Belfast.

Thoughts on the future

For the future, Miss Yousuf hopes that Northern Ireland will "retain the same level of tolerance and friendly relations" that have and do exist. The recent rise of racial attacks since the end of the 'Troubles' concern her as do the "troubling" reports of attacks on the Mosque since 9/11. She believes that more 'cross community' incentives would be a way forward but feels that the responsibility for initiating these must come from both the wider community and the Muslim community.

Appendix 1

Dear Friend

I have been commissioned by Al-Nisa to research an exciting new project which aims to publish a book celebrating the achievements of Northern Irish Muslims and to recognise their contribution to Northern Ireland Society. It is also planned to include a chapter on the History of Muslims in Ireland which is being written by Dr Khan.

I am writing to invite you to take part in this project or, perhaps to nominate someone else whom you feel should be included in the book. It is planned that the book will include entries from 20 men, 20 women and 10 children and young people. It is hoped that the book will be representative in terms professions, academic achievements, involvement in the community and the country of origin of the participants or their parents/grandparents.

We also wish to include participants who have been born or brought up in Northern Ireland but who are now living elsewhere, particularly if they still have links with Northern Ireland.

If you are willing to be included in the book, I would be grateful if you could provide a photograph either by e-mail or by post (I will scan and return any photos sent). Alternatively, I could arrange to meet with you to take a photograph.

Please could you also provide a contact address so you can be sent an invite for the launch of the book?

If you would like any further information about the project, please contact me.

Questionnaires may be returned to me by e-mail or by post.

Thank you for your interest in this project and I look forward to hearing from you.

Yours faithfully
Moira McCombe

Appendix 2

QUESTIONNAIRE FOR BOOK ABOUT NORTHERN IRISH MUSLIMS

Personal Details

Name: ....

How would you prefer to be referred to in the book?
(i.e. Mr, Mrs, Miss, Ms, Dr or by your first name):

Age: .... Gender: ....

Country of origin of self or family: ....

Profession: ....

Family members (e.g. children, spouse - optional)

....

....

Address (to send invite for launch):

....

....

....

Contact Telephone Number: ....

Times we can phone you: ....

May we phone you for further information? ....

May we include you in the book? ....

Background

What do you see as your professional/academic achievements?

....
....
....
....

What is your involvement in both the Muslim Community and the wider Northern Irish Society?

....
....
....
....

If you were originally from another country, when did you move here and what made you decide to settle in Northern Ireland?

....
....
....
....
....

What has been your experience of living as a Muslim in Northern Ireland?

....

....

....

....

....

....

....

....

....

....

What would you see as your hopes for the future relationship between the Muslim Community and the wider society in Northern Ireland?

....

....

....

....

....

....

....

....

Glossary

BA	Bachelor of Arts Degree
BIC	Belfast Islamic Centre
BMA	British Medical Association
BSc	Bachelor of Science Degree
ECDL	European Computer Driving Licence
DRCOG	Diploma of the Royal College of Gynaecologists.
FRCS	Fellowship of the Royal College of Surgeons
GP	General Practitioner
HND	Higher National Diploma
MCRC	Multi-Cultural Resource Centre
MA	Master of Arts Degree
MBBS	Medicine Bachelor & Bachelor or Surgery
MPhil	Master of Philosophy
MRCGP	Member of the Royal College of General Practitioners
MRCP	Member of the Royal College of Physicians
MRCPath	Member of the Royal College of Pathologists
MSc	Master of Science Degree
NI	Northern Ireland
NICEM	Northern Ireland Council for Ethnic Minorities
NIIF	Northern Ireland Inter-faith Forum
NIMFA	Northern Ireland Muslim Family Association
NIPPA	Northern Ireland Pre-school Playgroup Association
OFMDFM	Office of the First Minister and Deputy First Minister
PhD	Doctor of Philosophy
Plab	Professional & Linguistic Assessments Board
PSNI	Police Service, Northern Ireland
SEELB	South Eastern Education & Library Board
UK	United Kingdom
WEA	Worker's Educational Association

Eid	The annual celebrations marking i) the end of the fasting period (Ramadan) and ii) the end of the time of pilgrimage (Hajj)
Halal	That which is permissible for Muslims (e.g. Halal Meat - this has been killed in accordance with the rules of the Islamic faith.
Hijab	An Arabic word that describes Muslim women's entire dress code, including the veil.
Ramadan	The annual period of fasting
9/11	The attacks in New York and Washington on 11th September, 2001
7/7	The London tube and bus bombings on 07th July, 2005